Gathering The Fragments

By

Sue McClish Melton

Forward

Gathering the Fragments is a collection of stories from my family history. This is a collection of family stories, it is NOT always the facts, just the stories that have been passed down thru generations by those who have gone before and those who believe them to be true. To paraphrase a title from a friend of mine's book, this book could be called "Legends, Lies and other cherished Myths of McClish family history".

Years ago I got asked "Who do you think you are?" It wasn't said to be nice but as an insult. Well today, I would like to think, I know who I am. I am a mixture of cultures and family that span decades. It took a lot to make me and now I want to share that side with you.

I started this journey because I asked my Dad about people whose surname was the same as ours. I had asked him if they were related. Very few times did he say yes, mostly he said "I don't know." So as a curious pre-teen, I started collecting names. I used to love looking at my mother's record book and in the front there was a "pedigree chart." I tried to copy that so I would have some sort of pattern to what I saved. Needless to say, it was a lot of work, and got a bit confusing. However, I continued on.

Over the years, I have gone from those first steps, to getting some help from a lot of people, in the form of letter writing, personal record searching (this means traveling to court houses and searching in dusty records also), and now using the internet to collect these stories.

My younger brothers and sister did not have the opportunity to get to know our Great grandmother (**Alma Albertha Glines Solomon**) or our Grandmother (**Flossie Esther Trowbridge Brattain Line**) as they died before they were old enough to have the opportunity to know them. So in a way this is a book for them so that they can get to know "Who they are." I hope this gives a small picture of our family tree. Some of the stories are downright funny and others are surprisingly historic. But mostly they are to allow us all to know that those who have gone before us were just ordinary people with a story to tell.

So Sit back, enjoy the journey of "Gathering the Fragments" of our history.

Sue McClish Melton
August 2018

William Everett McClish

This adventure starts with my Dad. He wasn't a large man in physical appearance; in fact, he was five foot, eight inches tall and weighed one hundred thirty-five pounds. He was a giant in my eyes.

This picture is one of my favorites because Dad only had the opportunity of wearing that uniform officially for eleven days. He so wanted to be in the military. He had family that served in WW II and he wanted to be just like them. I wonder sometimes what his life would have been like, had he fulfilled his dream.

Company 2516, Clover, Utah. September 1938
Civilian Conservation Corps

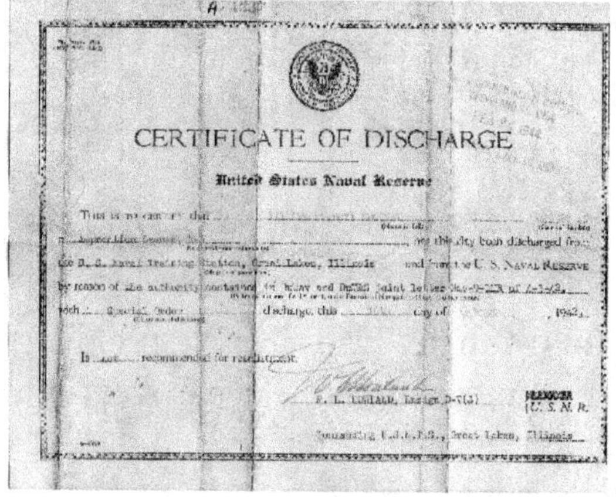

Dad served six months in the Civilian Conservation Corps in Utah and when he returned home, he had been encouraged by his cousin **Bud Solomon (Ernest Everett Solomon)** to join the military. His choice was the U.S. Navy. He was sent to Great Lake Naval Base for his basic training. While he was there, he got malaria, and as a result the Navy released him. That was eleven days after he had joined. Since this was in the time of War, he is considered a WW II Veteran.

Dad taught us all to respect the military, our flag, our President and our country. We did not dare disrespect any of those things. He loved our country and considered himself lucky to have been born at the time he did. He wasn't rich in money but rich in the things that meant the most.

Dad was born to **George Washington McClish** and **Olive Alice Solomon McClish** on 15 August 1922 in Durant, Holmes County, Mississippi. From all I have read, he was a normal baby. His mother, was as hard working as his father. His mother was not as strong as she should have been after giving birth to my father and she developed Tuberculosis. She died 1 April 1924, just eighteen months after giving birth to my dad.

Grandma's mother and father (**Fielding Bailey Solomon** and **Alma Albertha Glines Solomon**) came to Mississippi to help move the family back to Indiana. While doing so, they divided the children up among siblings and other family members with the exception of Dad. He was too sickly for anyone to take on....sooooo with the determination that Grandma **Solomon** possessed, she said she would raise my dad. From what I have gathered thru family stories, Dad was placed on a pillow and carried back to Indiana, not expecting to live.

But with the love of his grandparents, he thrived.... One of my favorite pictures was taken when he was two and half years old.   He does not appear to be happy that his picture is being taken but the look on his face was typical of Dad's look. Unfortunately,

there is no one that I can ask, regarding the
background of this picture. I can only imagine it.

This picture was
obtained from my
brother, who is also my
Dad's namesake,
**William Everett
McClish Jr.** I don't
know how he came to
have it, but I am glad he
did. A small bit of my
dad's history that we
were not aware of and
able to preserve, thanks
to my brother's saving nature.   I still think he was
cute.

There is really little known of Dad's childhood but one
story he told me when I was younger gave me a little
incite into his relationship with his Dad.

From all indications, **George Washington McClish**
was a loving but hard man to know. He died when
Dad was about eight years old, so the memories are
few, but with that said, there is one story that stands
out.

Dad said that as a young boy, he was always curious

how things worked. One day he took apart his father's watch. Instead of getting mad at dad, Grandpa told him that since he took it apart, he could put it back together again, AND IT HAD BETTER WORK. Dad said he did put it back together and it did work. Others have said that Grandpa was a man who said things once and once only. You had better listen when he told you something because he was not fond of repeating himself. I think Dad acquired some of that because that was how I was raised.

It seems that at times Dad lived with some of his siblings because one of the stories I heard was regarding him throwing his nephew out a window. This occurred when dad was staying with his brother, **Julius Edson McClish**. It seems that **Julius Jr.** and Dad were tussling and got a bit rambunctious. Dad flipped **Jr.** over him on the bed and **Jr.** flew out the window. I asked **Jr.** if they got into trouble because of this and he said they did not. How they got out of it, will remain a mystery.

While staying with his brother, one time dad was given money to take him and his nephew to the movies..... well dad didn't want **Jr.** hanging around (probably because he had a girlfriend or was wanting to pick up girls) so he ditched him. **Jr.** said that he got even, he shellacked the seat of dad's bike and when dad got on the bike, he got stuck and tore the seat of his pants out getting off. **Jr.** said he had never seen dad so mad. (I can imagine).

Dad was raised Salvation Army. **Grandma and Grandpa Solomon** were devout members of the Corps and Dad was raised accordingly. I think this is one of the reasons he was so caring about people. He was a hard man sometimes but underneath he was surprisingly gentle.

Dad met my mother when she lived in New Castle, Indiana. I am not sure how they wound up living together because, after dad's death, mom came to each

of us kids and told us that dad and she never married.
I am sure that **Grandma Solomon** had something to
say because of her beliefs. It is possible that she
"kicked" dad out of her house when she found out that
mom was pregnant with my older sister. I am sure
that Grandma was disappointed in dad, as he was her
precious "little boy." I don't think Grandma ever
approved of dad living with a married woman with
three small children and not divorced yet.

Dad had a way with animals. On one of the farms, we
had a rooster. This rooster hated my mother and my
older sister for some reason, but Dad and I could
chase it all over the yard and it would never bother us.
He was the basis of several adventures and many
stories. (I might devote a chapter just to him.)

Dad seldom laughed out loud but on one occasion
(much to my sister's
embarrassment) I thought
he had totally lost it.

My sister (**Alice Ann
McClish**) had a problem
with the rooster that we had
on the farm. He would
attack her every time she left
the house unless, she had
some sort of protective
weapon (in the form of a

broom or shovel) with her. This one day, she left the
house and ran to the outhouse (we did not have an
indoor bathroom at the time). In doing so, she left her
weapon behind. Dad saw this, so he watched from the
living room window to make sure that she got safely
back to the house.

Dad said as he watched, **Alice** opened the door and
looked out. He thought she was going to come out
right away because, so far, the coast was clear, no
rooster. "Well," he said, "she closed the door" and as
he watched she waited for a few minutes, and opened
the door. Right there at the door, was, you guessed it,
Mr. Rooster.   **Alice** slammed the door on the rooster's
neck and started screaming "Help me! Help Me! I
can't get out!"

My mother and I were so startled when we heard dad
start chuckling and then laughing so hard that he
nearly fell over on the floor. He finally got himself
under control and went and rescued his oldest
daughter from that dragon rooster. Needless to say
Alice learned a valuable lesson that day... not that she
didn't try to forget a weapon... but then thought better
of it.

That outhouse was the cause of another "rescue" from
my dad. I was about five years old when another
"dragon" appeared and dad came to the rescue. I
never liked the idea of going to the bathroom in a

chamber pot, UNTIL, the day the monster dragon appeared to me, in the outhouse.

One night I had to go pee so bad and I didn't want to use that chamber pot, so I ran out to the outhouse. I opened the door and went inside only to be met by two green eyes looking at me from the hole where I would have to sit. I turned and ran from the outhouse back to the house. By the time I got back to the house, I no longer had to pee.

Dad checked the outhouse and the only thing he found was the possibility that an opossum had gotten in there and that was "the dragon with the green eyes." My dad, my hero.

Dad was a hero again when he observed a ruckus in our chicken house. He picked up his shotgun and went outside and fired one shot. Dad went out to retrieve his bounty when low and behold, he shot not one, but two groundhogs who were disturbing our chickens. I thought he had to have been a super marksman to have accomplished such a feat. Years later, I realized that a shotgun shell scatters when fired so to have killed two was not something that was that unusual. But Dad still remained a sureshot in my eyes.

We usually went on vacations, somewhere. One year, when I was about five years old dad decided to go to

Salt Lake City, Utah. He had been stationed near there when he was in the CCC and wanted to go back and see some of the things he missed.

On the trip we went to Canon City, Colorado. Dad had ridden a train from Ft. Benjamin Harrison, Indiana to Salt Lake City, Utah. On this trip he had traveled at the bottom of the the Royal Gorge. He vowed that someday he would see this canyon from the top. He elected to do this when I was five years old.

The suspension bridge is 1,053 feet above the gorge... to a small child that it a very loooooooooonnnnnnnngggggg way to fall should the bridge not hold up. Dad decided it would be fun if we walked across the bridge. We did, but I held on to all my stuff and mom like glue. I figured she was large enough that she would not fall thru the cracks. I vowed that day, NEVER to come back to this bridge and I have kept that vow. I have seen it in the distance a couple of times but NEVER again up close and I never want to. This little adventure also created in me, a fear of heights.

I remember the day my dad came in and announced that we would not be taking any more long vacations.... the reason...gas had gone to twenty-five cents a gallon.

We did take more vacations but one of the games we played was to see if we could spot the cheapest gas prices as we traveled. Usually we would find a gas war and get gas very cheap. The trip to Salt Lake City was the longest trip that we took, while I was growing up. Dad took several more after I left home.

My dad and I did not always agree but I still loved him. One of the adventures that I recall, was a time that dad forgot his lunch. By this time we had moved to Marion, Indiana and dad was working at Paranite Wire and Cable on South Adams Street. We had one car and dad had taken it to work. We discovered Dad had forgotten his lunch pail. I told mom that I could walk the distance and take it to him. We had had a bad snowstorm, so the streets were not in the best shape and the weather was cold and the buses were not running. I bundled up and proceeded to walk to his place of work and take his lunch.

I got to Paranite ok, a bit cold but ok. I took dad's

lunch to the personnel office and asked them to give it to my dad. While I was there, the enterprising young lady that I was... I tried to sell some of my doormats that I was manufacturing in Jr. Achievement. I did sell a couple. This was my way of allowing myself to warm up before starting my way back home.

The weather got a bit colder while I was in the office so when I started back, I got to Needham and Sons Funeral Home and went in to warm up a bit more before starting again. Well, one of the guys who worked there suggested that he take me home. Since he was a classmate of mine (and cute), I said ok. I did not realize that he was going to take me home in a hearse.   I can only imagine what Mom must have thought, when she saw that hearse pull up in front of the house. She wanted to know what was going on since it was a young boy that brought me home and in a hearse, no less.

Dad worked at Paranite for several years. Thru all that time he was very careful around the machinery.   His job was to make wire. One day something caused him to be distracted from his normal routine. As a result, he attempted to unloop a piece of wire while it was going thru the machine. The wire wrapped around his finger and tore the end of his middle finger off. This was the only accident he had in all the years he worked there.

As a result of his working for Paranite Wire and Cable, he became fascinated with electricity. I was about ten years old when we got our first TV. In those days you had what was called a "tuner" and periodically it had to be cleaned or it didn't work right. You usually had to call a TV repairman to come out and do the job. Well dad figured, if that guy could do it, dad could learn to do it too. So he found out what he needed to do and started doing the work himself (this was not unusual for Dad). One day he was looking at the back of the TV and he saw a box on there that said "Do Not Open". Dad, being dad, decided he wanted to know why he shouldn't open it. He started to open it and we heard a great big "POP" and saw dad flying across the room. His comment..." Well, I guess I know now why I shouldn't open it.!" That was Dad.

Dad had a green thumb... no matter what he planted, it grew. On the farm we always had a garden. Dad and us girls usually took care of weeding it and watering it. Mom took care of "putting it up for the winter". There was nothing like fresh produce. One of my favorite things was to pick a tomato and eat it right out of the garden, or sweet corn freshly cooked. I miss those things today. We even had a garden when we moved to Marion. Dad saw to that.

As I stated before, Dad and I did not always agree but he respected my decisions. He stood up for me when I wanted to join The Church of Jesus Christ of Latter

Day Saints. I had to have permission as I was only sixteen years old. Mom was opposed to it and dad said yes. He told mom that it was better that I be associated with a church than not. She begrudgingly gave permission. I was baptized on the 8th of August 1965. My parents did not attend and that was something that saddened me a lot.

When I got married to **Edward Eugene Justice**, and as we were preparing to move to Enid, Oklahoma, dad made the remark that nothing important could happen in the month of May because the traffic around Indianapolis was so bad that we would not be able to get back. Well dad died the 12th of May 1980. He might not have thought it important but I did. By this time, I had divorced **Ed** and married **Harry Leroy Koehn**. **Harry** could not take time off work to come to dad's funeral so I decided to take my two oldest boys and travel back for the funeral. Dad and I had not spoken to each other because of a situation regarding my brother **Paul**, BUT I did respect him and mom and to not go to his funeral would have been unforgivable.

Enid Genevieve Brattain

My mother was born 12 February 1920 to **Charles Emmitt Brattain** and **Flossie Esther Trowbridge Brattain**. She was the youngest of their five children. The first child **Bertha Hildred Brattain** lived only about 6 weeks. She died of "organic heart problems". Not sure what that means but that is what is listed on her death certificate.

Enid Brattain, Taken at Clifty Falls Park 30 Oct 1938

Mom was a complex person, as many of us are. She refused to use her middle name because that was not the name listed on her birth certificate. It was however listed as such in the Brattain Bible. Interestingly enough no one's full name was listed on her birth certificate.

When mom was just twelve years old her father passed away from pneumonia. This bothered her more than she wanted to admit. All of her siblings were grown and she was the only child at home. She had been very close to her father. She told of stories of sitting at his feet reading crochet instructions to him as he crocheted. These crocheted pieces would eventually be shown at the County Fair under her mother's name because her father would not admit to doing this woman's work. Many of those pieces found their way into mom's life. She preserved them and used them cautiously around the house. She herself, could do some pretty work. My sister, **Brenda** also has that talent.

One of her favorite things to do was to embroidery. This was one of the skills she taught all three of us girls. She was a perfectionist at this work. If our work did not meet her standards, we would have to take it out and do it again.

Sometime around 1932 mom was introduced to singing on the radio.   In an interview I did with Mom on Feb 15, 1998 and she told me that she started playing the guitar professionally at the age of 12 and played until shortly after she married **Don Ellis**. The people who started her playing were **Earl Dean** and his son **Wayne Dean** from Fairmount, Indiana.

This was mom's guitar now in the possession of **Brenda Lee McClish Brown**.

One of the stories that mom told was, one night she was singing and playing the guitar at the National Barn Dances in Cincinnati, Ohio. In the audience was a man by the name of **Red Foley**.   The MC brought **Red** up on stage and asked him to sing a few songs. **Red** chose the guitar that mom was playing that night, to use. From that day on mom was a big fan of **Red Foley**.

Mom was a jealous type. I have been researching our family because of my dad being an orphan, but when I would try to ask him questions, mom would ask, what I was doing for her side of the family. I have worked on her family as well and showed her the information. She never did want to see what work I did for dad.

Mom married **Donald Oris Ellis** on 31 May 1939. She met him thru her "show biz" connections. This marriage produced three children. From all indications, this was not a very happy marriage and while **Don** was away, both strayed from their marriage vows.

Enid Ellis Taken 3 Aug 1942

At one point **Don** went into the Army Air Corps. The only stories that mom ever said, were stories that were not very complementary to him.

Sometime in 1943 she met **William Everett McClish**. She was still married to **Donald Ellis** as they did not get their final divorce until 1 Oct 1949.

Alice Ann McClish
ca. 1950

From the time she met my dad, until the divorce was final, she had two more children. My sister **Alice Ann** was born 9 July 1944 and I was born 7 Oct 1948.

Mom always told us that we would never know when she and dad married.   When my sister and I were younger, we used to ask her how she met my dad. She would never tell us and then say, we would never find out when they married. My older sister and I wanted to do something special for their anniversary and that was the response we were given. Dad never said much.

It wasn't until after Dad died that Mom came to each
of us and told us that she and Dad never married. She
said she tried to get him to marry her but he never
would. I don't know his reasoning as he stayed with
her for so many years.

I do know from a story that my **Aunt Frances** told
that at one point Dad and Mom were going to split up.
This was after I was born and before my sister **Brenda**
was born. They went to Missouri to talk to **Aunt
Frances** (this would be my Dad's sister) about
adopting both of us. My Aunt said that she took my
dad aside and told him that he brought us into the
world and that he had a responsibility to raise us.
That he did not have the right to "give us up" So that
ended that discussion from what I am told.

On that visit to Missouri, **Aunt Frances** told me that
Mom had an encounter with a Billy goat. It seems that
mom made the mistake of bending over and presenting
her backside to the goat and he took advantage. He
butted her and knocked her face down on the ground.
Aunt Frances said it was really funny but my mom
did not think so. I asked mom about this one time and
of course she denied it.

Mom and Dad must have had a hard time because,
after I was born, there were five children in the
household. From the stories I have been told, mom
was not a good mother to the three older children. Her

means of punishment were cruel. I don't know what
the circumstances were but more than one person has
indicated that she would sit one or more of the older
children in first hot then cold water for punishment.
Because of this, she eventually lost custody of the
children. She eventually transferred the blame to me,
saying that it was my fault that she lost custody... that
had I not been born, she would still have them. I was
not even two years old when all of this custody change
came about. She never admitted that she was cruel to
the older kids.

Over the years I have been in contact with two of my
older siblings and enjoy the idea of having a big sister
and big brothers. Sometimes I don't think they think
so but it is a warm spot in my heart just to know they
are there.

It is not my goal to present a picture of mom as a bad
person. In 1997, I came back to Indiana actually to
get married, BUT things did not work out and I
eventually decided to have mom live with me and take
care of her. She was in a nursing home, just sitting
there, crocheting and I wanted to spend some time
with her.

I had been away from Indiana for approximately forty
years and I figured it was time to "come home". The
sad part was that mom did not have her home to go to.
When she went into the nursing home she deeded the

house that dad bought her, to my sister, **Brenda**. It seems that my ex brother in law, my older sister and my youngest brother, took advantage of a loop hole and forced **Brenda** to allow them to take all of mom's possessions from the house. It was supposed to go into storage but none of it made it there. Many of mom and dad's possessions were lost due to this maneuver on the part of those involved.

I decided that she could live with me. I would take care of her and I had hoped that some of my siblings would visit as well. They decided that since I had mom with me they would ignore us both. The only person that tried to involve herself into this relationship was my Aunt (mom's sister). She had been told stories regarding me that were untrue and she did not like the idea of mom living with me.

During the two years that mom lived with me, we had some adventures. She loved to read and her favorite author was **Zane Grey**. She also loved **Gene Stratton Porter**, so on a whem, I decided to take her to the **Gene Statton Porter** Museum in Geneva, Indiana. I loved her books too and thought this would be a fun time for her. While at the museum, mom found that her two favorite authors had been friends and had lived neighbors, on Catalina Island in California. She was so excited to find this tidbit.

While in Berne, we decided to stop at Amishville Café and have lunch. I told mom to order whatever she wanted. She didn't seem to know what to order, so I helped her to order Spatzel, I, on the other hand ordered an Apple dumpling. I had been craving one for a while. While we waited for our order, we enjoyed the bread and apple butter that was there on the table. When our order came, Mom looked at her plate and started eating and enjoying her meal. She looked over at my bowl with my Apple dumpling and homemade ice cream and took her spoon and stole my ice cream. I was so surprised. She just sat there with that innocent look on her face as though saying "what did I do?"

The waitress saw all of this and started giggling... and I just looked up and said "can you believe that? My mom stole my ice cream!" We all got a good laugh out of that.

Mom was a complicated person to know. On one hand she could be a lot of fun and on the other hand she could be the meanest person you ever wanted to know. During the time she lived with me, I tried to make sure the time was good. We did a few fun things and she seemed to enjoy those times.

I still had my connections with some of my entertainer friends and on one occasion, I was asked to go with one group to New Bern, North Carolina. I explained

that I really wasn't available as I had mom to take care
of. They said to bring her with me. So we traveled to
Nashville, Tennessee and met up with The **Hammond**
Brothers, who had a bus to go to New Bern. Mom had
never been on a tour bus. She and I got to sit in the
back where normally the lead person stayed. Mom
could not settle down to rest but she did enjoy the
adventure. The **Hammond**s were opening for one of
mom's favorites, **George Jones**.

We got to the venue and I got mom seated up front so
she could see the show. I told her I had some work
that I had to do and that she was to stay there. The
bus driver kind of decided to look after her, so that
freed me up to do my job. This was the first live
concert mom had ever gone to. Oh she had been a
performer but had never sat in an audience to see the
performance. I think it must have triggered something
in her mind, because as we traveled back to Indiana,
after leaving Nashville, to go home, she told me to take
her to her mother's. When I told her that her mother
had died in 1960 (this was 40 years before), she got
upset and told me to take her to her brother's place. I
told her that I couldn't do that as he too, had passed
away. She really got mad them. She stated that I sure
knew a lot about her family, when I was not even
related to them. She had lost all recognition of me. It
was then that I knew she had Alzheimer. When we
got home, my friend who had looked after the house
while we were gone, told me to "duck". I did and just

missed getting hit in the head by mom. I knew then that she had to go back into the nursing home. Our time together had come to a close.

I have some special memories during that time I spent with mom, and I don't regret taking the time. In the end she didn't know me but there for a while she was the mother that I had always dreamed of, the one that loved me.

She also got to meet my favorite author, **James Alexander Thom**. He had just written "The Red Heart" and we went to his book signing. She had never been to one and had never met an author in person. When **Jim** found out that she was a **Brattain**, he told her that in his next book, there was more about a man named **Bratton** that was a part of the Lewis and Clark Expedition. Unfortunately, mom died before that book came out.

During the time mom stayed with me, we had a few "health scares". We discussed what would happen when she died. I told her that when she died that I would not attend her funeral. She said she understood. I told her the reason why, was because of the way things worked out at dad's funeral. I told her that I could not go thru that again. She understood.

One time, I had to take her to the emergency room and she nearly died on me then. I told her that if she died I

would put cali lilies on her grave. She hated those
flowers. She pulled thru that time. She also asked me
if I was serious about the flowers. I told her yes. She
said she was going to stick around cause she did not
want them on her grave. Well in October 2000 she
passed away. It wasn't until several years later that I
was able to return to Indiana, and I put a cali lily on
her grave. I kept my promise.

The Emmetts

I have grouped the Emmett families together because there are several stories involved. When I first joined the Church of Jesus Christ of Latter-Day Saints, I was given to understand by my family that I had done something that no other member of my family had done. I had gone and become a MORMON. Well as it turns out there were quite a few members of my family that preceded me. I had some early Church pioneers in my family. Some were not so nice but still they are a part of my family and a part of this history.

James Emmett

James Emmett was born 22 Feb 1803 in Boone County, Kentucky to **Silas Emmett** and **Elizabeth Trowbridge**. He joined the Church of Jesus Christ of Latter-Day Saints in February 1831. He was an active participant in the early efforts to establish the church in Independence, Missouri and served at least once as a missionary to his native Kentucky. He was briefly disfellowshipped from the church for unwise conduct in 1837 while he was in Far West, Missouri. In 1839 he was reinstated in time to share with his fellow believers, Governor **Lilburn W. Bogg**'s incredible "Extermination order" which demanded that the Mormons be expelled from Missouri or exterminated.

For the next five years he played a supportive, if inconspicuous, part in developing the new Church center at Nauvoo. Though prominent leadership posts eluded him he was eventually appointed to the "General Council" an influential political advisory committee to **Joseph Smith** . This council eventually gave advice to **Joseph Smith** on his candidacy for the Presidency of the United States in 1844. It also gave information regarding the future relocation of the chuch in the West.

In 1844 in a meeting with **Joseph Smith** and others of the council, **Emmett** volunteered to assist in exploring areas west of the Rockies for a new and safer site for the church and to preach the gospel among the various Indian tribes of the region. Before the prophet could personally direct such an expedition, he and his brother, **Hyrum** were murdered in a Carthage, Illinois jail. **Emmett** was assigned to be one of the body guards to bring the brothers bodies home to Nauvoo for burial.

Emmett became uncomfortable with **Brigham Young's** tightening control over the church and decided to implement his own understanding of **Joseph Smith's** February commission to explore the West. He decided to leave Nauvoo before any possible apostolic intervention could take place. He planned to persuade as many people as he could to follow him and secretly head west into the wilderness.

In the summer of 1844, following the death of the prophet, many pioneers feared an escalation of the hostilities and persecutions. **Emmett** capitalized on this and feigning authority from the Twelve Apostles, he convinced several of his associates to follow. His instructions were to "break up (break camp) and remove immediately to the West, without passing thru Nauvoo," but to go to Fort Madison instead. Many of the gathered peoples did so because they thought that he was carrying out the orders of **Brigham Young**. The truth was that **Emmett** was acting without authorization.

.

On 4 September 1844 **Emmett**'s group went quietly and quickly across the Mississippi River above Nauvoo. They made passage by wagon and flatboat through Fort Madison and Burlington, the **Emmett** company sold their flatboat for additional teams and wagons and traveled one hundred fifty miles northwest up the Iowa river before setting up winter quarters seven miles northwest of Marshaltown in Marshall county, Iowa.

By this time **Emmett** had seized complete and arbitrary control over the group, and was exacting uncompromised allegiance. He was espousing an economic order and theology that alienated a growing number of his followers. He ordered the surrender of ALL private properties, including beds and oxen, and called for public ownership of everything. Evidence indicates that **Emmett**'s orders extended to include wives and children. According to members of the group who left, **Emmett** was proclaiming himself as **Joseph Smith's** true successor, perhaps a peg or two greater.

Two disaffected followers later wrote: "**Emmett** searched the camp and confiscated all guns and threatened everyone with death if they opposed him."

Unknown to **Emmett** and to the rest of the Twelve Apostles, **Brigham Young** had known all along when and how **Emmett** would leave and what his plans were. **John L. Butler**, while acting as one of **Emmett's** chief lieutenants, had kept **Young** secretly informed. **James Emmett** did not fare well in his new role. **Amasa Lyman**, one of those dispatched in late February of 1845 to visit the **Emmett** company in person, reported near starvation, forced compliance and inequitable distribution of food, clothing and other resources. Such events and reports were sufficient for **Brigham Young** to denounce **Emmett** as an "intelligence of the wilderness," one who was wild in his own imagination of power and authority. It was becoming clear that **Emmett** was unpredictable and that he might cause as much, if not more trouble among the Indians as he had among the Saints.

With **Brigham Young's** plan to remove the Saints
from Nauvoo, his concern was that **Emmett** could
either foolishly or deliberately, stir up Indian
animosities against the migrating Saints.   Even if this
did not happen it was possible that **Emmett** could still
provide all the grist that Church critics in Washington
D.C. might need to further their claims, that the
Church would ally themselves with the Indians and
exact murderous revenge on the Missouri frontier
towns and overland wagon trains.

During the summer of 1845, **Emmett** had a change of
heart. He returned to Nauvoo, conferred with the
Church authorities, pled for forgiveness and sought a
full reinstatement in the church. **Brigham Young**
treated **Emmett** surprisingly leniently, perhaps wary
that a humiliated church frontiersman could cause
great problems for the Saints among the Indian tribes.
However, even though he reinstated **Emmett, Young**
was too shrewd to trust him any further.

This was not the end of **Emmett**'s skullduggery.
While the two men who were assigned to go with
Emmett back to Fort Vermillion, prepared to return to
Nauvoo, **Emmett**'s unreliability surfaced. The two
men agreed to sell their horses to a local French trader,
whom they named **Brewyer**. **Emmett** tried to nullify
the sale. **Brewyer**, incensed at this intrusion,
persuaded his father-in-law, **Chief Eagle** and the
Chiefs of nearby tribes to attack **Emmett**'s camp. The

attack was averted at the last moment through the intercession of a French-Indian friend of old **Chief Eagle**. The man pled for mercy and promised to get **Brewyer** his horses. The two men left **Emmett**'s camp on 3 October, leaving **Emmett** in charge.

Eventually, **Emmett**'s wife disowned him and his followers distanced themselves from him. **Emmett** was soon after disfellowshiped from the church for disregarding the counsel of the church. **Emmett** tried to convince his ex followers to go with him to California. He stated that they could do much better there. One of his previous followers went with him. His daughter. He died in San Bernardino, California in obscurity in early 1950's.

Another story found regarding **James Emmett**:

If you are interested in the truth, PLEASE READ the following and let this man's memory be full of facts and not memories of elderly persons who were only retelling stories they heard, and never witnessed. He never led his family to the poor camps across the river from Nauvoo, he was far away, traveling in Indian country toward what became Vermillion, South Dakota.

James Emmet was an early member of the Church of Jesus Christ of Latter-day Saints. He was born in Boone County, Kentucky, married **Phebe Simpson**, and had a family of twelve children, only five of whom lived to adulthood. From the time of his baptism in 1831, he eagerly followed the LDS Church wherever the leaders asked he and his family to go. He served as a missionary in Illinois, Indiana, Kentucky, Ohio, and Missouri. Asked by **Joseph Smith**, the Prophet, to explore routes westward and take the Book of Mormon to the Iowa Indians, he did so in September 1844. **James Emett** never claimed to be a spiritual leader of anyone or any church. He did not leave the Church, he left his family in the capable hands of his oldest son, **Moses Simpson Emett**, who conducted the family to Utah in 1850. **Charles C. Rich**, Apostle, recorded in his diary that he collected tithing from **James Emett** in the gold fields of California. **James** died at age 49 in and was buried in Cottonwood Cemetery, Cottonwood, Shasta, California.

22 Feb. 1803–28 Dec. 1852. Born at Boone Co., Kentucky. Son of **Silas Emmett** and **Elizabeth Trowbridge**. Married **Phebe Simpson**, 13 Apr. 1823. Baptized into LDS church, 1831, in Boone Co. Moved to Jackson Co., Missouri, by Apr. 1832. Ordained an elder, by Sept. 1834. Served missions to Illinois, Indiana, Kentucky, Ohio, and Missouri, 1835. Stockholder in Kirtland Safety Society. Moved to Far West, Caldwell Co., Missouri, by 1837. Member of Far West High Council, 1838. Moved to Adams Co., Illinois, 1839. Moved to Lee Co., Iowa Territory, by Apr. 1841. Appointed to Iowa Stake High council, Lee

Co., 24 Apr. 1841. Moved to Nauvoo, Hancock Co., Illinois, by Dec. 1843. Appointed to Nauvoo police force, 29 Dec. 1843. Appointed by **Joseph Smith, Jr.** to explore western U.S. and identify new location for Latter-day Saints, 21 Feb. 1844. Admitted to Council of Fifty, 13 Mar. 1844; rejected from council, 4 Feb. 1845. Led advance party of Latter-day Saint members from vicinity of Nauvoo to vicinity of present-day Vermillion, Clay Co., South Dakota, 1845–1846. Moved to Waubonsie, Fremont Co., Iowa, by Apr. 1847. Migrated west to Salt Lake valley, 1849. Traveled to the Gold Fields of Northern California. Died at age 49, buried in the Cottonwood Cemetery, Shasta County, California

http://www.josephsmithpapers.org/person/james-emme tt. You will find all manner of errors in Church History, JS papers, family history accounts of his travels west with his family, including tossing the family bible from his wagon, Keeping his wagon loaded in Utah for a time and then when his family decided to stay in Utah, left in a huff and went to CALIFORNIA.

As I stated at the beginning, there are several stories about our family.... this is an example of that. Just remember I am "gathering the fragments" and letting each reader draw their own conclusions .... I just want to preserve these wonderful memories for those who come after us.

Lucinda Emmett

Lucinda Emmett, daughter of **James Emmett** and **Phoebe Simpson**, was born 25 April 1831 in Cook County, Illinois.

When **James Emmett** decided to go to California, after hearing about the gold rush, he concluded to leave his wife and two small children with the Saints in Council Bluffs, Iowa and take **Lucinda** with him. She had been his help since she was four years old. His two older children were married and the next oldest had passed away. He figured **Lucinda**, now eighteen year old would be a big help to him in making a new home.

This was a great trial for **Lucinda** and her mother.
They had buried five babies out of the seven in the past
few years. They now had **Marinda,** four years old
and **Sara,** five months old. These trials, along with the
persecutions and trials of the Saints, served to knit the
love of mother and daughter more closely together.
When **Lucinda** was told of her father's decision to
take her to California, her rely was "Mother, I can't go
and leave you and the babies."

What made her trial much harder was, she was very
much in love with **Sanford Porter Jr.** and had
promised to become his wife as soon as he was
released from the Mormon Battalion (Company E).
She felt that her father was unjust to ask her to give up
all that was near and dear to her, even her young
friends and girlish pleasures, and make her home in a
new country, mostly inhabited by Mexicans and
Indians.

She said, "Mother, I am going to run away and hide
until father goes." Her mother answered, "My girl,
don't you realize that with your father's temper and
determined disposition, that he won't go until he finds
you. Go in peace, praying that God will bless and
comfort you."

Soon after they left and started across the plains to
California. **Lucinda** walked and drove two yoke of
oxen. They stopped in Salt Lake City a few days to

rest. It so happened that the Mormon Battalion was discharged in the spring of 1849 in California and **Sanford Porter Jr.** arrived in Salt Lake City a few days ahead of the **Emmetts.** On hearing that they were in town, he went to see **Lucinda,** thinking she would soon be his bride. When he spoke to her father about it, her father asked, "Do you believe in polygamy?"

Porter answered, "Yes, but it would be up to her if I practiced it." **Lucinda**'s father answered, "My answer is no, and you just as well go."

This was such a sad parting, after **Porter** was gone, **Lucinda** felt so bad that she broke down and sobbed and cried. This worried **James** and angered him until he picked up the whip and whipped her.

After reaching California, **James** looked around for a few days. He finally decided to file a homestead in San Bernadino. He built a cabin and a chicken coop. He then sold one yoke of oxen and bought a cow and some chickens. Having no farm implements, they grew watermelons and squeezed the juice out through a coarse cloth, boiled it down and made syrup to sell.

A few months had passed and **Sanford**, still sad and lonely for the girl he loved decided that she too was lonely and unhappy. He made up his mind to go to California and find her. His efforts failed, so he concluded he would try and forget his love for her and hoped she would do the same. He married about two years later.

Later **Lucinda** was told of **Sanford's** search for her. She said she guessed it was a good thing he didn't find her as she was so unhappy and miserable, she didn't know what might have happened.

James became very "cranky". Nothing **Lucinda** did seem to please him and as time went on, the future didn't get any better.

One time her father accused her of destroying his choice watermelon seeds and lying to him about it. He gave her such a severe thrashing that afterwards her back was so sore, she couldn't bear to have anything touch it. In order to protect her back, she wore one of his old shirts. He found later that a rat had carried his seeds away. Another time, she had a felon (*A painful purulent infection at the end of a finger or toe in the area surrounding the nail. Also called whitlow.*) on her finger that pained so badly that she could not sleep. Her father told her she could boil juice. Early the third morning, the felon broke, the pain left and she fell asleep and let the syrup burn. He whipped her for it.

James told her that if he ever denied the Book of Mormon, she would know that he had apostatized (*an act of refusing to continue to follow, obey, or recognize a*

religious faith). He denied it a while before he passed
away on 28 December 1852. He was her father and
she felt bad about his passing, but still felt her heart
rejoice that she was free to go back to her loved ones.

Lucinda found it took what money that she had to pay
for the doctor and funeral expenses. She couldn't sell
what little she had for enough to pay for her traveling
expenses. She learned that by living on the land for
fifteen more months, they would allow her to prove up
on the land and get the deed. She could then sell it and
get the money to take her back to Iowa. After she
decided to live on the land and until she could get the
deed, she sold the other yoke of oxen for money to live
on.

She found she was very lonely. For months at a time
she would not see another white woman. She would
often sit beside her house with strong field glasses and
watch the activities of the Indians camped nearly a
mile below on the river bottoms. One day she
witnessed a burial. She said the Indians took the body
of their dead brother, placed his head between his
knees and tied him in that position. They then passed
a rawhide rope around and around his body until he
resembled a large ball. They rolled him into what
appeared to be a newly dug well. They then killed his
horse and dog and threw them into the well after him.
Next they threw in his gun, blankets and some acorns

and filled the remaining space with dirt.

She said the Indian children were punished for disobedience or misbehaving by having a mark placed on their foreheads telling the length of time they must go without food, and no one dared to feed them until the parents had removed the mark and fed the child.

She found that she needed some help and company, so she sent to the nearby Indian village and got a very dependable child to be with her. She soon learned to love him.

One day she sent him to the store and he came back with a book. He said "White boy let me take the book, he looked over store door and read where to buy sugar and over another door where to buy shirt. I can't read. I want to learn like white boy. He say, you will learn me. Will you?" **Lucinda** replied, "Yes, **Peter**, I will be glad to."

In early spring of 1854, **Lucinda** received the deeds to her land. She sold the land to a neighbor and began to prepare for her journey back to Iowa.

Peter said, "I want to go with you, ask momma I can go." They ask his mother twice, but she wouldn't give her consent. When **Lucinda** bade him good-bye, he cried like his heart would break. She didn't feel much happier leaving him.

Her journey took her by steamship along the Pacific Coast then a steamboat up a large river as far as that went, then the rest of the way by stage to Council Bluffs, Iowa. She had been in California for five years and had heard nothing from her mother. She was disappointed that they were no longer in Council Bluffs but was pleased to find they were all in Utah.

A company of Saints were just ready to start for Salt Lake City, so she got to come with them by driving an ox team across the plains. When she arrived in Utah she found that her mother had become the second wife of **Sanford Porter Sr.** Lucinda went on to Ogden to live with her sister **Mary** and her husband **Armstead Moffett. Lucinda** became **Armstead**'s second wife on 9 Apr 1855. This union was blessed with five boys and two girls. Both girls and one of the sons passed away in childhood.

In 1885 **Lucinda** adopted an orphaned girl who was very sickly, having heart and lung trouble. She nursed her back to health and in the spring of 1891 the girl married **Lucinda**'s son **Robert**.

Armstead Moffett died 27 March 1891. **Lucinda, Robert** and his family moved to Star Valley in 1896 and settled in Smoot. **Lucinda** went to visit her son **Ammon** and his two families about two years later.

In the night of 15 August 1901, **Lucinda**'s sixteen year old grandson, **Junius**, was killed by lightening. **Lucinda** returned home the next summer and went to live with **Robert** and his wife **Mary**, who was not well. **Mary** passed away about three years later, leaving five children, between the ages of two and twelve, in grandma's care. This was a great responsibility for a lady of her age, but she never complained. **Lucinda** passed away on 20 July 1916. Her life had not been easy. It seemed she was blamed and accused of many things that she did not do or could not help. She never spoke unkind words about anyone, but always in a feeling of love for all. She passed away loved and respected more by those who knew her best.

Lucinda's younger sister **Sarah Catherine** (who was born 12 December 1848 in Pottowatomie County, Iowa), married **Lyman Wight Porter** as his second wife, on 18 March 1865. They had three sons, **Mortancumer, David Wight** and **Jared Lyman. Sarah** died on 6 July 1896 in Porterville, Utah.

James Simpson Emmett

Ironically, one of my mother's favorite authors was **Zane Grey**. Little did she know the man she loved to read, was influenced by an ancestor of hers.

Zane Grey came to the west in 1907. During his several months in the canyonlands of the Utah-Arizona border, he learned on the one hand to love the awesome beauty of the wilderness and on the other hand to love **James Simpson Emmett**, his responses to both were to provide matter for all of the novels about Utah that was to follow.

The significance of **James Simpson Emmett** has been missed, even though **Grey** made several references to **Emmett** in his books. In 1926 an article for the *American Magazine*, referred to the Mormon cowboy as "The Man Who Influenced Me Most". **Emmett** was the principal shaper of **Grey's** views on the Latter-Day Saints. **Emmett's** influence is seen in many of **Grey's** works, including *The Heritage of the Desert* and *Riders of the Purple Sage.*

James Simpson Emmett was born 28 July 1850 in a covered wagon on the Mormon Trail. At the age of sixteen he left the family home in St. George and went north to build Fort Hamblin at Mountain Meadows. On 2 April 1872 he married **Emma Jane Lay** in Santa Clara, Utah and took her to Hamblin. At age twenty eight, Emmett was hired to be Superintendent of the Canaan Cooperative Stock Company. He then moved his family to Kanab, Utah where he purchased fifteen acres of land and became involved in church and community affairs. In 1888 he was on the Board of Trade and in 1889 he was the Marshal. His residency in Kanab was interrupted for six months in 1881, when he served a church mission to the Southern States. In 1891 **Emmett** moved to Orderville (about twenty five miles to the north). Five years later, **Emmett** moved again to Lee's Ferry on the Colorado River for the Church. The work there was varied. **Emmett** operated the ferry, of course, and recommended improvements. He also worked to generate a tourist trade in the area and enjoyed the good land of **John D. Lee**'s old farm. He ranged widely as a cattleman and guide. Sometimes too widely. He was returning from a trial in Flagstaff where he had been accused of rustling, (he was aquitted). (He was oppositional to the Grand Canyon

Cattle Company when they fenced public land and he cut the fences for his cattle to graze. They tried to charge him with Cattle Rustling but it didn't stick.) While in Flagstaff he met **Grey** in 1907.

It was no wonder that such a seasoned pioneer of the Church's frontier should impress **Zane Grey**. **Grey** listed four ways in which he was affected by **Emmett**. The Latter-Day Saint, he said, taught him about bravery, about love for the desert, about kindness to animals and about endurance. **Emmett** could no doubt be discussed under each heading. A more fruitful approach, however, is to see **Emmett** as a specific inspiration for **Grey**'s Church characters, both the heros and the villians.

According to **Grey, Emmett** did not look heroic. "He stood well over six feet, and in his leonine build, ponderous shoulders and great shaggy head and white beard gave an impression of tremendous virility and dignity". He had no fear of any man...he feared only his God.

In the historical conflict between the two groups (Mormons and Gentile) there had been violence. South of Kanab (Utah) **B. F. Saunders** and his Grand Canyon Cattle Company started to put pressure on **Jim Emmett**. In 1880 **Saunders** bought land in Paroshant Valley; within three years his riders were trying to jump **Emmett**'s springs in Cane Beds (on the east of

Little Buckskin Mountain) and before long the conflict was perennial. In 1907, for example (the year of **Grey**'s trip to Utah) there were attempts to muscle **Emmett** out of grazing rights in House Rock Valley, and it was a matter of public speculation as to whether **Charlie Dimmick, Saunders**' foreman would kill **Emmett** or **Emmett** would kill him.

(**Grey**'s discription of **James Simpson Emmett**) **Emmett** was not greedy; he did not exploit his fellows (rather, **Grey** reported, he was himself exploited by them); when, some years before the **Emmett** brothers had been at the heart of "a nest of cattle thieves" in Kanab, **James Simpson** had not been one of them. Nor was **Emmett** lustful-if his monogamy was anything to go by (and for **Grey**, it probably was).

In 1909, having lost his long fight with **Saunders** (the Church of Jesus Christ of Latter-Day Saints had sold Lee's Ferry to the Grand Canyon Cattle Company), he took his family to Annabella, purchased land there, and helped to incorporate the town. By the time **Emmett** died (in Hinckley, in 1923) **Grey** had published several tributes-direct and undirect-to the man he had loved. Their number, their range, and their typicality amongst **Grey**'s fiction are evidence that **Emmett** was indeed the man who influenced him the most.

My comment: *I do enjoy reading **Zane Grey**'s books and after researching **James Simpson Emmett's** life, I plan on rereading some of them. More importantly, I have a copy of "Mountain Meadows Massacre" by **Juanita Brooks** as well as **Levi Peterson's** book, "**Juanita Brooks**". Both of these detail history of Southern Utah and a lot of the history of the Church during that era. **Zane Grey** wrote fiction, but it was based on some parts of history of the Church of Jesus Christ of Latter-Day Saints. A history that overshadowed the true nature of the religion. Some people chose to ignore the good and dwelt on the bad about the people that had been driven from the USA into the wilderness, why, because they chose to "worship in freedom." The United States supposedly was built on freedom of religion... but from all research, it meant only, if agreed upon as being like mine. Clearly the Church of Jesus Christ of Latter Day Saints, was not like others. Therefore (in some minds) it had to be stopped. I admire my ancestors in their quest to survive in a hostile atmosphere. They did what they felt was right. Not all agreed, it is obvious, but they lived a simple life and only wanted to be able to develope a community that believed in God as they saw him.*

Rev Jacob E. Gillespie,

Jacob Gillespie was born in Sumner County, Tennessee, in November 1809.

In 1826 when he was just seventeen years old, he was apprenticed to a man in Franklin, Tennessee to learn the tanner's trade. When he was about eighteen years old he was converted and joined the Presbyterian Church during his three years of apprenticeship.

He married **Almyra Hanna** in 1831 and on October 18th 1831 he moved from his place of birth to LaFayette County, Missouri with his young wife. Here he joined the Cumberland Presbyterian Church. In

1832 he became a probationer for the ministry, placing himself under the care of Lexington Presbytery, at a meeting of which **Rev. Samuel King**, (one of the founders of the denomination) was moderator. He was licensed and ordained by the Presbytery, his ordination occurring at a meeting of Presbytery in Independence, Missouri.

During the first eighteen or twenty years of his ministry **Mr. Gillespie** traveled and preached extensively throughout that part of the State in which he lived.   He preached the first sermon ever preached in Harrisonville, Missouri, the town then consisting of a few log cabins.

In 1852 he joined a company composed of eight wagons, of which he was chosen captain, on it's way to far-off Oregon, crossing the plains without any incident worthy of note save those hardships to be looked for on so long and perilous a journey. On the 9th of September of the year, this party camped on the Clackamas river in Oregon, when **Jacob** continued his journey direct to Lane County, purchased the donation claim of **Abraham Peek**, on which he took up his residence on October 6, 1852. This tract is situated one mile north from Eugene City, and has for one of its boundaries the beautiful Willamette River. Here **Mr. Gillespie** has continuously resided since that time.

In 1853 he organized what is now the First
Cumberland Church of Eugene. Since then he has
organized a number of churches among them is the
Church of Cottage Grove.

In 1857 he was elected one of the board of county
commissioners, and held that office until Oregon was
admitted into the Union as a state. While previously in
the session of 1854-55, he represented Lane county in
the Territorial assembly.

Mr. Gillespie married firstly, 4 August 1831 (some
records say 1 Aug 1831) to **Almira Hanna** and had a
family of seven children. He married secondly to **Mrs.
Amelia Martin** in 1845 and thirdly to **Mrs. Elizabeth
Goodpasture** on July 1857. She is also a Lane county
pioneer having settled within it's confines with her
former husband in the year of 1853.

 His daughter tells of his devotion to following his
Christian beliefs. She said that although her father
shaved regularly, all his mature life, she never knew
him to shave on the Sabbath but once. He was
detained from home, unexpectedly and he was asked
to preach a funeral. Until the infirmities of age began
to weigh upon him, he rarely missed an appointment to
preach, or failed to attend the meetings of his
presbytery or synod.

James Harvey Glines

The story of **James Harvey Glines** is being included in this book because it should be preserved for and by the family. **James Harvey Glines** in my opinion, is an important figure in the history of the American West. He was born on 17 April 1822 in Franklin county, New Hampshire to **James Pearsons Glines** and **Ruth Brown.**

When **James** was about two years old he was taken by his Uncle **Jonathan Fellows** to his home in the Northfield Factory Village for a visit. This eventually became his home. In 1832 **Johnathan Fellows** moved to **James'** father house in Franklin, New Hampshire. One year later they moved again to Peterboro, Hillsboro, New Hampshire.

James trained in the tailors trade and eventually
bought out **William Blair's** tailoring in Hancock, New
Hampshire. He carried on that business for a few
months and then returned to Peterboro.

James first learned of the Church of Jesus Christ of
Latter Day Saints in Lowell. Massachusetts, from **Eli
P. Magin**. On Mar 19th 1843 he was baptized by
Elder **Erastus Snow** and confirmed a member.
Shortly after he sold his business to **William Pratt** in
Peterboro. He traveled to Boston and then to Haverhill

James was one of the men appointed to campaign for
Joseph Smith for President of the United States.
Before he could make his first speech, word came that
the Prophet **Joseph** and his brother **Hyrum** had been
massacred in the Carthage Jail on the 27th day of June
1844. When he heard the news, he immediately
returned to Nauvoo, Illinois. He was taken into the old
police or what was commonly called **Joseph**'s Guard.
In this position, he guarded several members' homes
as well as the temple. This work was important
because there was a lot of unsettling events in Nauvoo
over the death of **Joseph Smith**. Many horsemen
were sent out to bring back to Nauvoo, families that
lived in outlying areas.

September 24, 1844 **James** went in company with the
Twelve Apostles, and President **Brigham Young**, who
had been arrested and charged with treason. He had

his trial and was cleared and discharged. They all returned the same day.

Governor's Troop entered Nauvoo on several occasions and searched several buildings. On the 8th of October the Governor's Troop broke up a conference being held for the Saints. As a member of the Old Guard, **James** was often guarding members of the church from harm.

On the 20th of December 1845, **James** married **Elizabeth Ann Myers** by Patriarch **John Smith**.

On the 8th of February 1846 **James** and his family, left Nauvoo and crossed the Mississippi river on the ice. They arrived at President **Brigham Young's** camp on Sugar Creek the next day. The camp commenced to traveling west and on the 2nd of March 1846, they were met by Capt. **James D. Allen** of the United States Army. He had come for the purpose of raising and enlisting five hundred men to serve one year in the Mexican War. These men were to be raised from the camps of the Saints. When the required number of men were raised, they were mustered into service on the 16th day of July 1846.

James became a father on the 27th day of October 1846, when **James Erastus Glines** was born at the Puncaw Camp two and a half miles west of Winter Quarters. On October 22, 1847, less than a year later, while **James** was on one of his trips, little **James Erastus Glines** died

James' second son, **George A. Glines**, was born on the 17th day of March 1850 at Harrises Grove, a place about twenty miles north of Kanesville. On the 13th day of March 1852 their first daughter, **Elizabeth Ann Glines** was born.

In 1852 they started for Salt Lake Valley in **Robert Wimmers** Company of one hundred wagons. They arrived in the Valley on the 4th day of October 1852. They stayed in the Valley until Feb 1853 when they moved to Cedar Valley about forty miles south of Salt Lake City. On the 27th day of Apr 1853 the whole settlement moved away from Cedar Fort to Lehi due to indian difficulties.

On May 18th 1854 **Charles Harvey Glines** was born and then on May 5th 1856, **Mary Jane Glines** was born.

James Harvey Glines passed away in Vernal, Utah on 31 August, 1905. He was laid to rest beside his wife **Elizabeth Ann Myers** in Cedar Fort, Utah.

Andrew Lawrence Glines

Andrew is the son of **James Harvey Glines** and **Elizabeth Ann Mayers**. He was an early pioneer to Utah being born just fifteen years after his parents moved to Cedar Valley, Utah. His mother died when was just eight years old. His sister, **Jane** was going to be married but when her mother passed away, she decided to stay and keep house for the family for a year. This help was needed because their father and two of their brothers were working buning charcoal in the West Mountains, leaving the younger sibling alone.

In 1883, his father and brothers made the decision to leave Cedar Valley and travel to Ashley Valley in Uintah County, Utah. They left Cedar Fort in two covered wagons, thru Provo Canyon over a toll road where they paid 25 cents for each wagon and 10 cents for each animal. One of the places they camped was Strawberry Valley, where the fish were so plentiful they caught them in burlap sacks. This trip took thirteen days.

After moving to Ashley Valley, it was fifteen year old **Andrew**'s job to herd the horses and cattle. **James** had made friends with **Old Tom**, the Chief, who gave them permission to keep their herd on the reservation. They kept the herd on the reservation during the summer and the badlands in the winter. For two years **Andrew** spent a lot of his time with the Indians. He was given the name "**Sackquitum**" which means "good boy".

One of **Andrew**'s brothers and **Ed Carroll**, took a contract to carry the mail from Ashley Valley to Green River, Utah. They hired **Andrew** to take the mail from Ashley Valley to the White Rocks Agency on horseback.   The mail and passengers, were carried by buckboard to Diamond Mountain. On one trip the horses were broncos and there were two passengers, a new Indian agent and his southern wife. She sat down in the wagon, he sat up on the seat. As soon as **Andrew** picked up the lines, the horses started with a lunge, the man went head over heels backward, off the seat and out of the wagon. The horses kept running for a mile or more before **Andrew** could get them under control and turned around to go back and pick up his passenger. His wife was hysterical thinking he had lost her poor husband.

The next morning they got to the rim of the mountain. Four miles from Brush Creek, the snow turned to rain. When they got to Brush Creek, the stream was very high, and they had to strap everything to the buckboard. When they left Brush Creek the soil was very slick and very slippery. The trip took them to Blue Hill which was the only way. Upon arrival the man got off the buckboard against **Andrew**'s orders and then grabbed the end of the buckboard, the horses slipped to their haunches, and they slid all the way down. When they got to the bottom, **Andrew** looked for his passenger and found him where he had slipped in the mud to his face and stomach. He was covered with mud from head to feet. Upon their arrival at Ashley, government men met them to take him over to the agency.

Andrew passed away 16 September 1960 , at his daughter's home in Salt Lake City, Utah. He is buried in Pleasant Grove City Cemetery, Pleasant Grove, Utah County, Utah.

George Albert Glines
and Mary Lundquist

George Albert Glines was born 17 Mar 1850 to
James Harvey Glines and **Elizabeth Ann Mayers**.
He was just an infant when his parents traveled to the
area of Utah. He was an early graduate of Brigham
Young Academy (later called Brigham Young
University). He loved music and played the violin. He
was also a boxer and a marksman with a rifle or a
pistol.

George and his wife kept President **Wilford Woodruff** in hiding for six weeks, because he was wanted by the law for being a polygamist. **Mary** made him a dress and an old-fashioned bonnet, and dressed President **Woodruff** up like a woman so he could go out and hoe in the garden for exercise.

George was also a foot racer. One time he won a cow and a calf for a man. Another time, while at a Fourth of July celebration a certain man kept heckling him, wanting to bet him that he could outrun him. Finally **George** said, "I'll tell you what I will do. I will run you a race one hundred yards, and will give you ten yards headstart. I will take this heavy belt and if I catch you I will whip you the rest of the way through." The man hesitated, the crowd yelled. "Good deal". The distance was measured off and the hesitate man found himself ten yards in the lead. He looked behind him and there was **George** ready for the race. The gun was fired and the race was on. **George** caught the man and whipped him for fifty yards while the crowd yelled their approval. After the race the man wanted to ship **George**, but was stopped by the crowd.

The story of **George** meeting his future wife for the first time is truly a love story:

When only thirteen year old **Mary Lundquist** was traveling from Bear Lake with Uncle **Peter Rasmussen** and others. They were camped in the

Strawberry Valley (Utah), where others were also camped. A man dressed in buckskin-fringed pants and shirt rode his tall back horse into camp. **Mary** became fascinated with the looks of that man with a black mustache and dark hair that was partly covered by a big hat, and dark eyes that seemed to smile with every word he spoke.

Even though he spoke in soft tones, everyone could hear and understand his voice. Some of the people who where camped there pronounced him as gentile, others didn't know. **Mary Lundquist** just kept quite. In her own mind, even though she was only thirteen she thought it would be nice to belong to someone, and this was the someone she imagined would be the right one.

That evening as she retired she asked the Lord about belonging to a good man. She had left Sweden when she was but ten years old, and had stayed with relatives and had worked hard for non relatives for her living.

Next morning everyone was in a hurry to get breakfast and get on the road, especially the **Rasmussen** relatives with whom **Mary** was traveling. **Mary** stood behind a bush to watch the man in buckskin-fringed suit mount hs horse. He started riding away, then quickly turned his horse and rode back. **Mary** found herself looking right at the dark eyes of the man in the buckskin-fringed suit. He waved good bye to **Mary**, who returned the salute, then rode away singing in his deep voice, "Israel, Israel, God is calling". **Mary** knew then he was no gentile. And with one question in her mind she climbed into the wagon and was on the road to Vernal.

The first Sunday **Mary** went to church in Vernal (Utah) the bishop announced the Brother **George Glines** would be the concluding speaker. Sure enough, this was the man she had seen at the camp in Strawberry Valley. Sometime after church she felt her hand in his and later on when she became fourteen years old her dreams came true and she became **Mrs. George Glines**.

Let me introduce you to my Material Grandmother. She is one of the reasons I started collecting information on my family. She was the one that showed me patience and consideration for any talent I might have. Since Mom really didn't like to teach me to cook, grandma often showed me how to do certain dishes. She was a lady that often was in my corner when no one else seemed to be.

One of my families all time favorite desserts was Bread Pudding. Now Grandma always fixed it without eggs because she was allergic to the yokes. So here is what she did.

Bread Pudding (Grandma style)

She would butter, heavily, a baking dish (size depended on how much bread pudding you were making.). Then she would put bread (this could be almost any kind of bread or bread product) that she broke up into a mixing bowl. She would add sugar (brown or white, it didn't matter) to taste. Then cinnamon to taste. She would then add enough milk so that the bread would get soaked completely (looked like a soggy mess). She would mix this all together and add enough vanilla to her liking. She would then place this mixture into the buttered dish and bake it for about an hour at 350 degrees until a slight crust would form on top of the pudding. This could be served hot or cold.

Sometimes Grandma would make a thin cornstarch pudding to be served over the top of the bread pudding. I can attest to the fact that the bread pudding could stand on its own. It was and still is, my favorite dessert. The real secret in this dish is the buttered baking dish. The butter would absorb into the bread as it baked forming a crust on the bread and adding flavor to the mixture. Atleast that was Grandma's theory… but I think it works.
Since we are on the subject of desserts. Another favorite was Rice pudding. Here is her recipe for that:

Rice Pudding (Grandma style)

Using the same set up as in the Bread Pudding recipe with the buttered dish (using about ½ stick of butter or margarine to butter a dish 9"x 13"). Place leftover cooked rice in a mixing bowl. Add cinnamon, vanilla and sugar (brown or white) to taste. Then add enough milk to make a soupy mixture. Place this mixture into the baking dish and bake at 350 degrees until milk is absorbed and a slight crust is formed on top (about an hour). This dish is best served cold so that it can set up.

Grandma married twice in her life. The first time was to **Charles Emmitt Brattain**. The story goes that Grandpa had gotten two girls pregnant and in those days, you married the girl you got "in trouble". So, he had his choice of the two and he chose Grandma. The first child was **Bertha Hildred Brattain**. She was born 13 Nov. 1908 and died 23 Dec. 1908. I do not know who the other woman was that Grandpa got pregnant. Obviously, there was another "**Brattain**" child but who that child is, is unknown.

An interesting note on the marriage of Grandma and Grandpa. On their marriage license Grandpa's name is spelled "**Brittain**". So, was that the correct spelling or was it a mistake on the part of the person who filled out the license? I tend to think of it as mistaken spelling because I have found him in other records and the name is spelled "**Brattain**".

After Grandpa's death in 1932, Grandma continued on the farm for some time. She eventually remarried to **Edson Burr Line,** the father-in-law of her son **Edgar**. She married **Burr** on 22 July 1944 and it was with mixed acceptance by her children, my mom in particular. Mom had just given birth to my sister, **Alice,** on 9 Jul 1944 so I can only imagine the

emotional turmoil she was going through when she learned that her mother was getting married to her brother's father-in-law.

As a child growing up, I got to know Grandma quite well but was restrained from knowing her second husband, **Burr** as Mom did not like him. He was a disabled war vet having served in WWI. He was in a wheel chair all the time I knew him and of course Grandma took care of him.

Grandma was an important part of my young life. I faced a lot of problems with being accepted by my mother and learning the things I should know. With mom, it was always "go ask your grandmother". Well now I didn't have my grandmother to ask. So, life began on a different level.

When I had to learn to make yeast breads for 4-H Grandma was the one who showed me how to make it. My second year in yeast breads, she encouraged me to to make cinnamon twists and I won a second reserve champion ribbon for my efforts. She was always encouraging me to do the things I loved to do.

I remember a time when I was about 5 years old. We went to see Grandma and Mom decided that I should "sing" for her. I have always loved music but know that I am tone deaf and cannot carry a true tune. I was so shy that I just couldn't sing. I mumbled thru it and Grandma came and gave me a hug anyway. She understood and kind of gave Mom a scolding for forcing me to sing when I was so shy. To this day, I cannot sing in front of anyone. I do love music and I do sing occasionally, but only for my enjoyment, not others.

One afternoon, Mom had gone to get eggs from a farm and noticed some exceptionally large ones. She mentioned that they were probably "double yokers", meaning that they had 2 yokes instead of one. She also said they would make good noodles. I asked her how to make noodles. She replied, "ask your grandmother. I can't teach you how because the recipe has to be handed down from grandmothers to grandchildren, not from mothers to daughters." So of course I asked Grandma how to make homemade noodles. This was her way of making them.

Grandma's Homemade noodles
1 egg beaten, add dash of salt. Mix in as much flour as you can and still have a dough. Turn the dough out on a floured board and knead until dough is no longer sticky. Cut dough into half and roll each half out as thin as possible. Leave on board until dough dries to "leather" consistency. Cut each half of dough into quarters and stack, placing a bit of flour between

layers so that the dough does not stick together. Roll into a jelly roll and cut into about 1/8 inch stripes. Shake stripes out and let dry again.

Noodles can be cooked immediately or placed in a plastic bag and frozen.   To cook Noodles, place in boiling stock for about 2 to 3 minutes. Fresh noodles cook quickly.

For the rest of my life at home, I made noodles every time Mom got a double yoker. When I left home and came back for a visit, she would always have double yokers on hand and I would have to make noodles so she could put them in the freezer and have them later. I actually got to the point of telling her that I would make the noodles if she would make a tuna noodle casserole that I liked. Believe it or not, she made the casserole. For a long time that recipe was lost so I didn't think it could be included in this book.

I eventually debunked the myth of the Grandma to granddaughters. I taught my daughter how to make the noodles and she does a great job of it.

Grandma's life was not easy, especially having to raise children on a farm. She was a single parent from 1932 to 1944. I know that she had some really tough times regarding my mother, as mom was very close to her father, but mom had married and had 4 children by the time Grandma remarried. It was time for Grandma to have someone to care for her and for her to care for. She loved her grandchildren but living alone, was something she really didn't want to do.

Grandma was a strict woman. She was quite religious in some ways. She believed in setting an example for her children as well as her grandchildren, in later life. You were always welcome there. She took in borders for a while and one such border, taught me "copper art". I always looked forward to working on the copper. My sister, **Alice**, and I did quite a bit of copper work with a man by the name of **George Marshall**. Where this man came from I don't know and I don't know his back ground, however, he did beautiful work on copper and passed it on to **Alice** and me.

I don't want to let on that all things were great in life, as one of the not so great things about **George Marshall** is that although he loved to teach copper art, he loved one thing more. He loved to molest little girls. I was one of them. I couldn't tell anyone because if I did, the art work would stop and I would be blamed for causing "trouble" in the household. I did attempt to tell my sister but she wouldn't listen and then tried to tell mom but she said I was making things up, so I kept quite and each time we went to Grandmas and **George** was there, we would do our copper art and he would fondle me. This went on for about a year. I was about 5 years old. At that time in life, I don't know if people really realized how molestation effected lives of children. I became even more withdrawn and wouldn't talk to many people. They called it "shy" but really was a kind of depression.

I don't know the whole story, but it was said that the house grandma owned in Fairmount, Indiana was offered to mom to live in. Mom turned the offer down. The house that is referred to was a large two story house right in Fairmount. My Uncle **Edgar** (Mom's brother) and his wife lived in Fairmount at the time and it may be that Mom didn't want to be close to family or that she didn't want to be in town, but she turned down the offer. Couple of things I remember about that house, is that in the kitchen there was an old cook-stove, the kind that you had to feed wood into. It was black and heavy as it was made of iron. The other was the front porch. I loved the front porch because you could sit out there and have friends over to talk. It even had a porch swing on it. It was the kind of porch I would still love to have. Eventually the house was sold. I think it has been torn down now.

My Grandmother was very special to me… I must give credit to her also for getting me started in working on my family history. I didn't work on Mom's side as much as I did Dad's but that was because, Grandma had given Mom a Family record book and in it was a Pedigree Chart that she filled out. There were places for Mom to put important dates going forward. I still use that as a source because Mom always kept newspaper articles to prove what was in the record. I learned how to create a Pedigree chart, so that when I found a name, I could get an idea of when they might fit into the family. My only regret is that I cannot recall the stories that Grandma used to tell us. They are lost now and that is one of my regrets and one of my reasons for preserving a written record of stores that concern the family.

I was told several years ago that what we take with us is a library, and when we died if we have not tried to preserve it… it is gone, forever. This is so true. When you think about it, you will also know it is true. There are days I wish my grandmother was still alive so I could ask her a lot of questions.

 On 17 May 1960, shortly before midnight, we received a phone call that Grandma had been in a car accident. She was coming home from a Rebekka Lodge meeting and a car had hit her. I remember the night because, mom woke **Alice** and me up saying they had to go to Marion to the hospital and that we were to stay inside until they came back. AND that ONLY **Alice** was to answer the phone. **Alice** and I were the two oldest at home. I was 11 and she was 15, my sister **Brenda** was 7, **Bill** was almost 3 and **Paul** was not even a year old. **Alice** and I were in charge of the younger ones. We got a phone call from Mom saying that Grandma had passed away just shortly before Mom and Dad got there. It was now May 18, 1960. My beloved grandmother had died. I felt so lonely because she had been so loving towards me. I could not imagine a world without my grandmother. To this day I sometimes wonder what life would have been like if she had lived a while longer. She wasn't that old but she was a very wise lady. At Grandma's funeral, (the first funeral I ever went to), they sang "How Great Thou Art". For the longest time when I would hear that hymn, I would start to cry. Grandma died 18 May 1960. That day changed my life. Grandma was buried in Estates of Serenity Cemetery, in Marion, Grant County, Indiana, USA. This still surprises me because most of Grandma's family is buried at Estates of Serenity, Marion, Grant, Indiana

This was taken Aug 28,1932. Left to right is Flossie Esther
Trowbridge Brattain, Cora Hane Veatch and Susan Jane
Trowbridge York.

Gas City Woman Dies Of Injuries Received In Marion Auto Crash

A Gas City woman died early today at Marion General Hospital as the result of injuries suffered in a two-car collision, making Marion's first traffic fatality for 1960 and Grant County's fifth.

The victim was Mrs. Flossie E. Line, 73, 527 E. S. "B" St., wife of Burr Line and a life resident of Grant County.

The accident occurred shortly after 10 p.m. Tuesday at the intersection of 26th and Gallatin Streets.

Her passenger, Mrs. Larma Pearson, 75, 3236 S. Boots St., received minor injuries and was released after treatment at the hospital. Driver of the other vehicle was Fred L. Silvey, 921 W. 26th St.

Dr. Henry Alderfer, Grant County coroner, said the death of Mrs. Line was due to a fractured skull. She was thrown from her vehicle in the crash.

Mrs. Pearson recieved abrasions of the right wrist and contusions of the right knee.

Mrs. Line was driving south on Gallatin Street, and apparently failed to stop for preferential 26th

(See GAS CITY, P. 3, Col. 1)

AUG. 26, 1960

Suit Filed In Fatal Car Accident

The estate of a Gas City woman fatally injured in a two-car collision at 26th and Gallatin Streets in mid-May brought suit in Grant Superior Court today for $15,000.

Edson B. Line, husband of the victim, Mrs. Flossie E. Brattain Line, has suffered damages in that amount by her death, the complaint states.

Defendant is Fred L. Silvey Jr., operator of the other car.

The complaint says Mrs. Line stopped her car at the one-way stop, saw nothing and proceeded into the intersection, where her auto was struck.

Silvey, it continues, was on 26th Street and his speed was neither reasonable nor prudent. The document charges he failed to keep a proper look out, failed to keep his car under control, and failed to yield the right of way. Silvey's speed was between 50 and 60 miles per hour, it charges.

The Twin City State Bank of Gas City is the administrator.

Suits Filed

CIRCUIT COURT

Carol Jo Willis vs. Boyd Carmen Willis. Annulment.

Marion Building and Loan Association vs., Wilbur T. and Sue Ann Smith et al. Note and to foreclose real estate mortgage.

SUPERIOR COURT

Betty Joan Waterson vs. William James Waterson. Divorce.

Darlene Reed vs. Charles Reed. Divorce.

Twin City State Bank, administrator of estate of Flossie E. Brattain Line, deceased, vs. Fred L. Silvey Jr. Complaint for damages.

ANNOUNCEMENTS

DEATH NOTICES

GOOD, ANORMA—216 S. Nebraska. Diggs Funeral Home.

OATESS — Corda. L. Washington Township. Diggs Funeral Home.

McNAMEE — Mrs. Addie L., 2705 S. Meridian St., Needham and Son.

LINE — Mrs. Flossie E. (Brattain) 527 E. South B, Gas City. Needham and Son.

LYTLE, Oscar C. — 219 E. Christy, Needham & Son.

Gas City Woman Is Crash Victim

(Continued from Page One)

Street. Silvey was driving east on 26th Street.

A native of Swayzee, Mrs. Line had resided in Gas City for 16 years. Prior to that time she had lived in Fairmount and near Point Isabel.

She was a member of the Gas City Christian Church, the Rebekah Lodge and the Ladies' Auxiliary of the Patriarchs Militant.

In addition to the husband, survivors are two sons, Edgar H. Brattain, Fairmount, and George N. Brattain, Wilmington, Calif.; two daughters, Mrs. George Blair, R. 1, Fairmount, and Mrs. Enid McClish, R. 3, Marion; three stepsons, Albert Line, Riverside, Calif.; Harry Line, at home, and Allen Line, Gas City; five stepdaughters, Mrs. Martha Belle Keffer, Pennville; Mrs. Mary Brattain, Fairmount; Mrs. Ruth Listenfelt, Fairmount; Mrs. Opal Barbour, Arlington, Calif., and Mrs. Wilma Phifer, Tipton; 22 grandchildren; eight great-grandchildren; 21 step-grandchildren. six step-greatg-randchildren; one brother, J. T. Trowbridge, Marion, and three sisters, Mrs. Birdie Overman, Kokomo; Mrs. Beatrice Crawford, Ithaca, N. Y., and Mrs. Susan York, Warren.

The body was taken to 814 S. Adams St. where friends may call after 7 p.m. today.

Funeral services will be held at 10:30 a.m. Saturday at the Gas City Christian Church. The Rev. Dewey Hole, pastor, will officiate, and burial will be here in the IOOF Cemetery.

McClish

The meaning of the name **McClish** is "Son of the Servant of Jesus". Many stories of how the first **McClish** came to America has floated around for years. Many families thought they were the last of the line, including mine. One story was that the **McClish** clan was run out of Scotland by the **McGregor**s and were supposed to be under the protection of **Bonnie Prince Charlie**. When he failed to show up at the dock where the clan was to board a boat for America...a fight broke out and all were killed except for one pregnant woman, who was hidden among the cattle until the boat safely left the harbor. This was supposed to have been the first **McClish** in America. However, in doing research on families here, my cousin **Shiela Sommerfeld**, disproved this story. It seems there were **McClishs** here before the Revolutionary war.

One story that is true is that **McClish**'s came from Scotland. Again there are stories that say they are from Ireland.... there is some truth in that. When the highlanders were driven out of Scotland by the British, some went to Ireland and remained there until they immigrated to America. These were then called Scots-Irish but the heritage was still Scottish. They were also known as "Planted Scots".

Some of our Clan did go to England. One such was
John McClish. While he was in England he was
shanghaied on a whaler, along with five of his friends.
He waited until he felt he could escape and when he
did, he was off the coast of Baja California. He and
his five friends, left the boat and made their way to
shore. Once on shore, he somehow convinced some
of the villagers to hide him. He took on the name of
Juan Augular.

 The following is from **Miguel Macliz**:

"As I understand it **Juan or John Macliz/McClish**
came over from England by way of a whaling ship. He
escaped from the ship off the coast of Baja California
and swam to shore and wound up in Santa Maria or
La Paz, Baja California. I've heard all sorts of different
stories on who, what, where, and when about the
Macliz or McClish clan but I really don't know what
to believe. My dad's name is **Ernesto Galindo Macliz**
and his siblings names are/were **Miguel**(deceased,
died in action WWII Batle of The Buldge), **Lorenza,
Francisca,Valentin**(deceased,Cancer just this year),
and **Consuelo**. I think there was another brother
named **Manuel** who died during childhood. My
father's parents names were **Valentin** and **Francisca
Macliz**. They lived in many parts of Arizona, Sonora
Mexico, and California. I know that my grandfather
Valentin was a miner and died from lung problems
due to working in the mines most of his life in San

Luis Obispo,California. in 1937. I heard that my grandfather loved to gamble and drink and of course womanize. My grandmother, **Francisca**, aka **Panchita**, died in 1983 here in Holtville, California. I guess the person that supposedly has a pretty good family tree documentation is my cousin **Richard Lozano**, son of **Francisca Lozano-Macliz**, he lives in Lake Elsinore, California. Although I hear it is supposed to be a pretty extensive family tree document, I myself can not vouch for it since I have never seen it myself.

Here is another version of the same story:

John McClish (b. ca 1797, Ireland) was press-ganged in England onto a whaling ship with 5 friends. They all escapcd from the whaling ship off the tip of Baja California by jumping overboard and swimming ashore near Santa Maria. There they were all rebaptized in the Catholic Church (my guess is about 1820).

 John McClish took the name of his new 'Godfather', **Juan Aguilar**. All 4 of his children were born with the surname "**Aguilar**". Later **John McClish** went back to his name but in a Spanishized version: **Juan Maclis(z)**. Most of his children did the same at some point. For instance at least some of the children of my husband's gr-gr-grandfather, **Juan Maclis** (son of **John McClish/Juan Maclis**), were born with the surname "**Aguilar**". A name they used their entire lives and their descendants are still known by this name. **Juan** later went by **Maclis(z)** and his later children were born with this name. [Confusing, I know!]

John McClish remained in Baja California until the Mexican American War. They supported the US Troops in the Baja during this war. In Oct 1848 the US Troops evacuated 340 persons from the LaPaz & San Jose del Cabo area of Southern Baja California to Monterey, Alta California because they were afraid of reprisals against these persons who had supported the American side in the war. **John McClish** and his family were among those evacuated. The **McClish** family stayed in Monterey for about 6-8 years then returned to their home in Miraflores, Baja California Sur. During their stay in Monterey, the Treaty of Guadalupe Hidalgo gave all the 340 persons American Citizenship. To remain Mexican Citizens individuals would have had to make an afirmative declaration of Mexican Citizenship. Without that they remained "Americans". I have not found any declarations for the **Maclis** family retaining Mexican Citizenship. So they went back to Mexico as "Americans"! Therefore all their descendants were born Americans even in Mexico!

John McClish's 2 daughters, Maria Pilar & Ysabel, married American Troops from the New York

Volunteers: Edward Kennedy married Maria Pilar, John Hearst married Ysabel. Edward was knows as "Eduardo Kenedi" and John Hearst was known as "Juan Corazon". These families lived in the Monterey, Alta, California and the Miraflores, Baja California Sur areas."

As descendants of highlanders, I was reminded that there were two lines that are supposed to be under the first "c" in **McClish**.... it is so right but I haven't figured out how to do that on the computer.

The history of the two lines indicate that the **McClish**'s were "line walkers". The **McClish** clan were highlanders from Scotland and as a line walker, they were the communicators between the peasants and royalty. So if you are not putting the two lines under the first "c" perhaps you should start as we have the right to that.

Lt. Col Edward Ernest McClish

This name is not familiar in many areas but (in my opinion) should be up there with the likes of **George Washington**, **John Adams** and any other patriot. Because of his actions 12 men escaped from the inescapable prison of Davao in the Philippines during WW II. A part of his story is told in the book "Escape from Davao".

He was a Choctaw. He believed in this country and he fought for it. From one of his sons, I received a bit more info on this man... He had a son who died in Vietnam and he did discourage his youngest son from joining the military, but taught him survival skills all the same. From this same son, I am told that even though he knew that the Japanese had killed and mutilated soldiers (including many of his friends) he retained a very high respect for them. I would like to think that this is because of his heritage. Braves respected Braves.

Chris (his son), tells me that his dad "at one point, had malaria and endured horrific fevers. He walked for miles through forest eating bark and bugs and was nursed back to health in a tribal hut-then once well, went back to fight."

His father was 60 years old when **Chris** was born. **Col. McClish** died in 1993. "He spent the latter years of his life in nursing homes and eventually an Alzheimer's unit."

I have to say, this is another of my HEROs in my family. Although I have not completed a link directly to me... I am proud of this man who shares my surname.

In this time of supporting our troups over seas, I am taking time to salute a true WW II hero. The sad part of this, is that he went unrecognized for so many years.

I am sharing just a little of what is written about him on the internet.

Like many of their fellow citizens, Indians have long served in the National Guard and Organized Reserve units in their respective States. **Lt. Col. Edward E. McClish**, a Choctaw from Oklahoma and a graduate of Haskell Institute and Bacone College, was called to, active duty in the National Guard in 1940 and sent to the Philippines. In 1941 he commanded a company of Philippine Scouts, then helped mobilize units of the Philippine Army and was commanding a battalion at the time of Pearl Harbor. Wounded and hospitalized on Mindanao in the early weeks of the fighting, he escaped capture and went underground to organize a guerrilla force.

By the fall of 1942, **McClish** had organized and armed some 300 men on Mindanao and consolidated his force with a similar one on the other side of the island. He then undertook to organize the guerrilla forces in the four eastern provinces of the island into the 110th Division. The organizational task was complicated by the presence of not only Japanese but of unorganized rival bands and bandit gangs. Potential soldiers also had to be educated as well as, trained. By the spring of 1943, **McClish** had organized three regiments and part of a fourth, and a division staff had been formed. To overcome a shortage of food and supplies, agricultural and industrial projects were launched throughout the division zone; vegetables and sugar cane and pigs and poultry were raised, and sugar, soap, alcohol, and coconut oil were produced.

When you think about the sacrifices that people have given for our freedom.... remember **Lt. Col. Edward Ernest McClish**.

Harry Marion McClish
Alma Rettie Knapp
Olive Alice Solomon
Mabel Lee

A letter from **Harry**'s son, **Lyle**, which tells of **Harry**'s life dated 20 Aug. 1994:

"**Harry** was born November 14th, 1891 in New Castle, Henry, Indiana. and dad told me when he was a small boy he became very sick and passed out. His mother and dad thought that he was dead and they covered him with a sheet. When the undertaker came to get the body he saw **Harry** move a little and they then called a doctor. Shortly after, he got well and continued on with his life. **Harry**'s mother, **Alma Retta Knapp**, passed away at the age of 34 years during child birth. **Harry** at the time was 6 years old and his father **George**, married again 6 years later to **Olive Solomon**. **Olive** passed away at the age of 37. **Olive Alice** was 16 years old when she married **George**. Home life wasn't the same for **Harry** and two years after his dad's marriage to **Olive** he left home. He was only 14 years old, but he wanted to begin life on his own. **Harry** stayed for awhile with **Oran Shoemaker** and was working at an auto company making Maxwell cars. **Harry** bought a small piece of land near a railroad track and built a shack to live in. When **Harry** was close to 20 years old, he decided that he wanted a better job to earn more money and improve himself. He bought a ticket to what he thought was Indianapolis, but instead the ticket was for Minneapolis. He arrived with little money in a big city.

Mabel Lee

Harry soon found work at a lumber company, so that he had enough money to live on. **Mabel Lee** and a girlfriend came from the county, a small town called Brook Park, which is located approximately 70 miles from Minneapolis, and they were working as cooks in a restaurant when they met **Harry**. **Mabel** encouraged him to study to be a cook and told him that he could make more money. **Harry** took her advice and soon had a job as a cook in a restaurant. An opening in a restaurant in Minot, North Dakota came up and **Harry** took the job. **Harry** wrote to

Mabel and her friend to have them come to Minot because there were better jobs with more pay. So **Mabel** and her friend left for Minot. A few years later, **Harry** had a chance to be the head cook at a hotel in Winnipeg, Canada and so he moved to Canada. After awhile **Mabel**'s friend decided to move back to Minneapolis and not long after **Harry** married **Mabel**, which was in 1912.

Harry and **Mabel** had a daughter, **Marguerite**, who was born in Winnipeg. **Harry** decided to move back to Minneapolis and he rented an apartment for himself and his family in Northeast Minneapolis and he started cooking at the Nicollet Hotel. Later he became the head cook at the Radison Hotel. **Harry** had a chance to become the assistant chef at the Minneapolis Athletic Club, which he took and he remained there for 30 years until he retired. **Mabel** was born on Jun 14, 1892 and passed away in Minneapolis in July of 1977.

All of **Harry's** sons served in the military service. All of the children of **Mabel** and **Harry** are very proud of their parents. **Harry** from the age of 14 years until 70 worked very hard and was a wonderful family man. **Harry** saw that his family had a nice place to live, had plenty of food and clothing and he never complained on working every day of his life. God had to be at **Harry's** side from the beginning of his life until he passed away at the age of 95 years and 24 days, which made him the wonderful family person over so many years". pg 234,235 McClish Kith and Kin.

(I met my Uncle Harry one time, as a little girl. As we were leaving, Mom wanted a picture of Aunt Mable and Uncle Harry, and as usual I was in the way of her picture. She told me to move and as she did Aunt Mable pulled me over to her and told Mom she had to take the picture with me in it. I don't know what happened to that picture but somewhere it is floating around in the universe.)

Arthur Lewis McClish

Arthur Lewis McClish was born in China of missionary parents, **Glade Leonard McClish** and **Sadie Chamberlin McClish**, and came to the U.S. when he was a year old. He attend schools in Indiana and after serving in the U.S. Army in Guam, graduated from the University of Illinois in 1947 as a landscape architect. Soon after graduation, he came to Seattle and worked for the Seattle School Board and then was director of the Bellevue Parks Department.

In 25 years with the federal government, **McClish** served as landscape architect and planner for the Federal Housing Administration and the U.S. Army. In the early 1970s, he opened his own office for landscape planning in Issaquah and later served three years as master planner with the U. S. Army in Germany. He was the first master planner at Fort Irwin, California, his last assignment before retirement.

McClish had lived on Cougar Mountain since 1960. He was an early member of the Pacific Northwest Cycling and was active in the Cascade Cycle group. He was a member of Issaquah Alps Trails Club and was active with barbershop singers. He was a former member of Issaquah Kiwanis Club and was a long-time member of the East Shore Unitarian Church.

Besides his widow **Glenna** of Issaquah and his mother **Sadie** of Tacoma, **McClish** leaves three children by an earlier marriage: **Mark** of Seattle, **Diane Gordon** of Carnation and **Carol Moser**, Renton; two sisters, **Myra McClish** of Arizona and **Lois McClish** of California, a brother **Leonard** of California and eight grandchildren.

Cause of death: Brain tumor.

John Venton McClish

John Venton McClish was born 13 Jan 1875 to **David McClish** and **Lucinda Nichols McClish.**

In his lifetime.. he went by several names, including **Benton, Vent, Vinty** and **Vint**, to name a few. His date of birth was changed many times as well. His actual date of birth is 13 Jan 1875.

According to family stories, **Vint** was in trouble with the law on several occasions. He married three times and on each of the marriage licenses there is data that changes from each time. Several times even the name of his wife changes but the date of marriage is the same... example when he first married **Rachel Norris**. Her name is shown as **Rachel Norris** or **Rachel Mock**... date of marriage is 8 Sept 1900.

His marriage to **Martha VanNetta** ended because he went to prison. I am not sure why he did but the record shows she divorced him while he was in prison. His marriage to **Sarah Clara Jenkins** is interesting because they say they have a child born in 1897 but they were not married until 1938. This birth of this child predates his marriage to **Rachel**.

Reubin Trowbridge,
Journal of Trek to California
Legend

The Journal of the trek to California included **Reuben Trowbridge** great-grandfather of **Evelyn Einspahr** together with his brothers **Henry Trowbridge** and **Sabin Trowbridge**. **Sabin Trowbridge** was secretary of the company and was therefore in charge of keeping the log.

Mrs. Einspahr generously allowed the Chase County Historical Society to copy the log and place it in the museum files.

CHASE COUNTY HISTORICAL SOCIETY NO. 424 LIBRARY DIVISION.

April 27, 1850
Council Bluffs

Constitution

Article 1. This Company shall be known as the Palestine Company.

Article 2. The officers of this company shall consist of a Captain, Lieutenent, Secretary, Sargeant, and Wagon Master.

Article 3. It shall be the duty of the Captain to have a
general oversight of the interest of the Company; to
form the order of march and in case of an attack from
an enemy to perform the duties of a military leader to
the best of his ability.

Article 4. It shall be the duty of the Lieutenant to
assist the Captain in his duties, when called upon, and
in his absence to perform the duties of Captain.

Article 5. It shall be the duty of the Secretary to keep
an account of the busines of the Company; to keep an
account of the distance of each day's travel.

Article 6. It shall be the duty of the Sergeant to call
the roll each day and to keep account of the time
when each man stands guard.

Article 7. It shall be the duty of the Wagon Master to
see that all are ready to start at the appointed time; to
report to the Captain any accident where necessary
repairs will cause delays, and to arrange the terms as
he may think proper.

Article 8. It shall be the duty of the officers of the
Company to select suitable camping gound and to
appoint the hour of starting in the morning.

Article 9. This Constitution may be altered or
amended at any time by a vote of two thirds of the
Company.

Voted to adopt the above Constitution
Voted to elect the officers by ballot.

Resolved that the officers of the Comapany shalll
serve four weeks.

Charles Frost	elected	Captain
E. M. Blair	"	Lieutenant
Sabin Trowbridge	"	Secretary
Robert Canady	"	Sergeant
Thomas Hopkins	"	Wagon Master

April 27, 1850

At a meeting called for the purpose of making
by-laws, the Company agreed to the following:

1. A committee of five shall be chosen to examine the
outfit of each individual and none shall be received in
the Company except such as have a suitable outfit.

2. All difficulties shall be settled by a jury of 12 to be
chosen by the Secretary; each party having the
privilege to object to any juror.

3. Each team shall take his turn in driving ahead and none shall be permitted to pass each other without the consent of the parties.

4. The Company shall not travel on Sunday except in cases of necessity. Also, that there be no target shooting on the Sabbath.

5. Voted that there be no discharging of firearms after the sentinels are stationed on guard.

6. Voted that no person shall molest or disturb an Indian unless they are the agressor.

7. This Company shall consist of not less than 50 or over 100 men and if the majority of the Company shall think it necessary to separate for the purpose of making greater progress, it may be done by the agreement of parties.

8. Voted that no loaded gun shall be put in the wagon except such as are uncapped.

Voted that **George Brady, Reuben Trowbridge, John Murphy, Crene Sawyer, Jesse Gray** be the examing committee.

Voted that the committee proceed to examination on Monday morning the 29th of April, 1850, and report at the next meeting.

The meeting is adjourned by vote of the Company.

April 29, 1850.

Committee reports, as follows:

Names of the individuals received into the Company and their place of residence.

From Lee County, Illinois

Charles Frost
Charles Hale
Henry Trowbridge
Alexander Gilmore
Stewart Stewartson
L.C. Sawyer
Charles Sawyer
Sabin Trowbridge
Thomas Hopkins
Reuben Trowbridge
G. A. Strickland
Joseph Carey
J.W. Carney
Nathan Howard
Franklin Roff
E.M. Blair
W. H. Blair
Adam Spalding
J. B. Morgan

Wm. Woodard
Wm. N. Knox
A. S. Ward
G. W. Cooper
John Hunter
Alpheus Walker
Joseph Thompson
Jesse Gray
James Sparks
George Hall
John Prouse
G. W. Grady
G. Parsons
Noah Strong
Abner Strong
Nelson Marsh
Calvin Marsh
J. R. Peters
R. Maxy
Eli Grosswait
 J.N. Walter
C. Maxy
Douglas Rutherford
James Rutherford
Ezra Bissel
Cyrus Brown
Anthony Wood
Abel Wood
James Martin
Moses Bissel

Henry Bly
Joseph Hough
James Thompson
Samuel Argraves
Thomas Mitton

From Marshall County, Iowa

John Murphy
Abbot Reed
John Leonard
George Astley
Joseph Birch
Joseph Murphy
Robert Kennedy
Wm. Kennedy
Wm. B. Sheffield.

The committee reported that the above individuals have a good outfit and that they be recieved into the company.

Crossed the Missouri on the 4th and 5th of May and camped one mile below the ferry on the river bank.

May 6, today we left the Missouri and traveled 12 miles and camped on a stream called Pappaum. Grass rather scarce.

May 7, Lay up today to let our cattle recruit.

May 8, Started and traveled over rolling prairie 16 miles to Elk Horn River. Crossed over and camped. Found tolerable good grass.

May 9, Lay still today to give our cattle a chance.

May 10, Started and traveled 8 miles over a flat and camped on the bands of the Platte.

Today a part of the Company were dissatisfied because of our slow progress and left us and now our Company numbers about 30.

May 11, Traveled about 16 miles. Camped by the side of a small lake. Grass poor.

Sunday
May 12, Made 12 miles over a very level country and camped on the banks of the Platte. Grass better.

May 13, Country still continues level without any timber except a very little along the river. Traveled about 12 miles.

For two days we have been in company with the Pawnee Indians much of the time. Sometimes they would travel with us for miles and be constantly begging, generally for something to eat, tobacco or money

Today at noon we were met by the Chief, an old man about 60 or 70 years old. He showed us a treaty which was made with the whites in 1825, and he had kept the documents in a good state of preservation. He gave us to understand that he was the white man's friend but he wanted us to give him something to eat which we did, and some other presents which pleased him very much, and then he told us that we were in perfect safety while passing through his tribe. We traded 12 quarts of corn for a good buffalo skin. The Pawnees are at war with the Sioux and dare not follow us much further for fear of them. I understand that they dare not even sleep on the north side of the Platte unless they sleep in a white man's tent or camp.

May 14. we have not seen an Indian today. Came about 12 miles over a level prairie of good farming land but passed through no tember. Camped by the side of a small pond of good water. Grass rather poor. Within the last three days, about 100 horse teams have passed us.

May 15, Made about 10 miles today. This morning we came to the Loup Fork. Forded the stream without accident after waiting about an hour or more to find a shallow place. This stream is about 50 rods wide interspersed with numerous sand bars and snags. The water is very shallow most of the way across and this river appears very much like the Platte.

May 16, Came 12 miles today. Followed up the
Loup Fork over a level prairie.

May 17, Came about 4 miles up the Fork and then
ascended the Bluffs and traveled 12 miles over
beautiful prairie. Camped on the bank of the Loup
Fork. No Indians in sight yet. The weather is very
dry and grass grows very slow but improves some.
Weather very dry and road first rate.

May 18, Left the Loup Fork again this morning and
struck across towards the Platte. Traveled over a level
prairie until about 3:00 o'clock. Found a little water
but no wood. Traveled on to find a better place to
camp but that place we did not find. We soon
ascended the Bluffs and continued to find nothing but
Bluffs and sand ridges for 10 or 15 miles further. At
last at about 11:00 o'clock at night we found a small
slouth with a little water in it but no wood. Camped
and turned out our cattle and we were tired and sleepy
and glad to get to bed. I suppose we traveled over 35
miles.

Sunday May 19, This morning we found good grass
and water for the cattle and buffalo chips to burn
which is the first time we have had to use them. They
burn first rate when dry,. Had a fine shower this
afternoon and some hail. This is the first warm rain
we have had this spring and now we expect grass in
abundance.

May 20, We passed over a level well watered prairie.
Traveled 20 miles and camped on a stream called
Wood River. Grass poor. Wood plenty.

May 21, Traveled over a most beautiful prairie.
KIlled a deer and camped by the side of one of the
best springs I ever saw.

May 22, Today we made 22 miles. Camped by the
side of the Platte once more in sight of the road on the
south side of the river, which is lined with teams.
Today we have seen buffalo for the first time but they
are very wild and I doubt our killing any very soon.

May 23, It has been a very warm day. Grass begins
to grow and the feed is getting tolerable good. H ave
made 20 miles. Level prairic--no timber except a few
willows on the streams. Camped on a small stream
called Buffalo Creek.

May 24, Traveled 20 miles today and camped on the
Platte. No wood except on the Islands, which we can
get by wading in shallow water.

May 25, Today has been a very exciting day. About
one half of our men have been hunting buffalo and
have seen thousands and killed a dozen and wounded
many more. Buffalo are very numerous and not so
wild as was expected and our boys have made
dreadful havoc among them today. We have seen

hundreds of deer over partly decayed and at first we
knew not what caused it but think that among so
many some must die daily, expecially in the winter
when exposed to cold and starvation. We came about
15 miles and camped to wait for the hunters to come
up.   Came up in the evening loaded with Buffalo
meat.

Sunday May 26, Today we moved 5 miles to get
grass. Camped on the Platte river near another
company. Found good grass. There is a Preacher in
the other company and they had meeting and most of
our company have been to meeting.

May 27, Last night we had a tremendous storm of
wind and rain. Blew some of our tents down and
most all of us got very wet. It cleared away in the
morning and we started and traveled over a low wet
prairie and made 26 miles. Some of the boys went
a-humting and killed a Buffalo and an antelope.

May 28, Today we had an election of officers, as the
term had expired several days ago. In the afternoon
we saw some Buffalo and half a dozen of us went
after them. Killed two of them and three of our men
got lost in the bluffs and traveled all night before they
got to the camp. Then teams made 17 1/2 miles and
camped near the Platte. The election is postponed
until another day.

May 29, Today we traveled over a sandy bluffy road
and camped near the Platte. No wood, and we do not
expect to have any for the next 200 miles.   Made 19
miles and camped near a small well of good water.
Grass tolerable good.

May 30, Today we traveled over some sandy hard
road in the forenoon but good in the afternoon.
Passed a number of good springs and creeks.
Camped near Rattle Snake Creek. Good grass. Came
20 miles.
Last night our officers were selected.
They are as follows:

E.M. Blair, Captain
Samuel Argraves, Lieutenant
Sabin Trowbridge, Secretary
Franklin Hoff, Sergeant
Thomas Hopkins, Wagon Master

May 31, Made 20 miles. Good roads most of the
way, Some sand ridges but generally level. Camped
near Watch Creek. Grass poor.

June 1, 20 miles over a level sandy prairie and nearly
destitute of grass in many places. Camped near the
river. Grass as good as we have found lately. Passed
a lone tree this morning and some ledges of rocks off
the road which are the first we have seen since we left
the Missouri. Some of our men have been over the

river this afternoon and have brought back some exciting news. Ther are hundreds of teams camped on the other side of the river recruiting but the grass is poor in the best of places and they are anxious to get over on this side of the river. Our boys have seen plenty of Indians on the other side of the river which are the first that they have seen for more than 200 miles.   They say they are rich Indians and belong to the Sioux.

June 2, Today we have passed a large number of Indian tents on the south side of the river but have been but two or three Indians on this side. The ground is covered in many places with a substance resembling saleratus (potash) and the water in many places is strongly impregnated with alkali. Made 17 miles today.

June 3, Today we passed the ancient ruins, so-called because they appear like such from a distance. They are nothing more than hugh rocks piled upon each other. We have 20 miles and found good grass.

We started this morning at 6:00 o'clock and made 23 miles. Last night we had a heavy shower of rain and after traveling a few miles, we found hail on the ground and continued to find it for 8 to 10 miles. The water had washed it up in heaps over a foot deep. Some of the hail stones were as large as prairie hen's eggs.

We are now traveling among the black hills. Had
rather a hilly but good road most of the way. We can
plainly see snow on Laramie's Peake in the Black
Hills 25 miles distant. Killed a black-tailed deer
today which is the first that has been seen. (The
"Black Hills" at that time extended down into what is
now Colorado, including the Scottsbluff area in West
Nebraska, where the caravan went past.)

June 14, Have been traveling over the Black Hills for
two days. We have come over some very high hills
and had a view of the surrounding country. It is a
regularly pleasing prospect and looks romantic.   The
hills are so high and steep that we can look from the
summits down into the tops of the highest pine trees.
Our roads today have been hilly but generally smooth
and good but were some rocky this afternoon.

Came 21 miles today and camped among the hills
with poor grass and no water except what we brought
along.

June 15, Yesterday we had a severe hail storm. It
lasted but a few minutes. Last night it was very cold
and windy. Today has been a very cold day and we
needed extra cothing to be comfortable. We have
made 20 miles today over mountainous road and in
some places rocky and rough. We are now camped in
the Black Hills. Have plenty of wood and water but
very little grass.

Sunday
Jun 16, We do not travel today but some of our men
have been a-hunting and killed two Buffalo, which is
worse than traveling on Sunday. These were the first
buffalo that have been seen for 300 miles.

June 17, Our teams have moved out of the Black
Hills today on to the Platte. Made 19 miles and
camped on a sand creek. Found a man going to the
States and says he will carry letters for 25 cents each
to the nearest Post Office. Some of us went to writing
and got ready to send them in the morning.

The river is very high and we have got to ferry it and
we have heard that it is impossible to get over very
soon at the ferry, which is 20 miles above here. The
rates of the ferrage are $5.00 for a wagon; $5.00 for
each yoke of oxen and $1.00 for each man, and we
have concluded that we will not stand it and think we
shall make a boat of a wagon box and ferry ourselves
as we did at Fort Laramie.

June 18, Today we moved down to the river. Made
our boat. Swam our cattle over, after considerable
trouble and by working till after midnight we got all
our things over except one wagon and two
wagonloads of goods without accident.

June 19, This morning we ferried over the rest of our
loads and started in good spirits, and came about 18

miles. Camped near the river. Found good grass and
a beautiful place to camp.

June 20, Three miles further we followed the Platte
and passed the ferry where there were five boats
constantly at work ferrying wagons, but people
generally swam their cattle and horses. The price of
ferrying is $5.00 per wagon and $4.00 for each yoke
of oxen, and $1.00 fore each horse or mule. We heard
that there had been 16 men drowned crossing at this
place, most of which were drowned swimming their
horses and cattle.

Here we left the Platte and traveled across a barren
country without any vergetation except wild sage and
wormwood. In about 12 miles we came to a mineral
spring and lake which is considered poisonous. We
stopped a short time but dare not turn our cattle out.
After resting we startd on and traveled 14 miles
further over a sandy barren country. Passed an alkali
spring and swamp. Could get no good water for our
cattle until night. We found a small stream of sulphur
water. Here we camped but all was gnawed off so our
cattle got none.

June 21, Started this morning at 2:00 o'clock for the
purpose of finding feed for our cattle. About sunrise
we found some very short grass. Turned out our
cattle to get what they could and we got our breakfast.
Traveled on over a barren country and after passing

alkali swamps and lakes and and quantities of saleratus, 24 miles brought us to the Sweet Water River. Found good water and some grass. We camped in sight of Independence Rock.

June 22, This morning we passed Independence Rock. It is about 120 rods long and 20 rods wide and I should think aobut 100 feet high. It is composed of granite rock, and is covered in many places with names and dats. Some of them were dated in 1843, but the great curiosity that we have seen yet we passed 5 miles from Independence Rock. It is a place called the Devil's Gate where the river makes its way through the rocks which are 400 feet high, perpendicular on the side next to the river but can be ascended on the opposite side with some difficulty.

We came 15 miles up the Sweet Water and camped on its banks. Found good grass. On our left on the mountain we can see plenty of snow 15 or 20 miles distant.

Sunday
June 23, We are laying still today in a beautiful and romantic place on the banks of the Sweet Water River. On our right, about a mile distant there is a tremendous pile of rocks composed of solid granite 500 or 600 feet high and extend as far as the eye can reach. The Sweet Water is a crooked stream about 4 rods wide and from 2 to 3 feet deep.

June 24, Traveled up the Sweet Water along the mountain of rocks on our right and on our left about 20 miles distant are mountains whose tops are covered with snow. We made 22 miles and camped near the river. Grass poor. Some of our men went a-hunting last Saturday. Some of them came in at 11:00 o'clock, one on Sunday and two did not find the teams until Monday afternoon. Some of our men think we ought to be called the mountain rangers.

June 25, We passed up the river. Crossed it four times in 10 miles. The water came into our wagon boxes and wet some of our things but not very much. Took them out and dried them. Made 26 1/2 miles and camped on the river and by going 2 miles down the river found tolerable grass. We passed an ice spring this afternoon and about one foot deep we found plenty of clear beautiful ice.

June 26, We have been in sight of the tops of the Rocky Mountains since yesterday noon and they appear to be covered with large quantities of snow. Today we have made 18 miles. Some of the way was over a very rough road. Found good grass.

June 27, Today we came 22 miles. Crossed the Sweet Water for the last time. Passed over several snow-banks, some of which were 15-20 feet deep. Camped within 4 miles of the South Pass on a high ridge among the sage brush. Rather poor grass.

June 28, This morning came through the pass over beautiful road. The shape of the land being some like that rolling prairies of Illinois but it is sandy and destitute of vegetation except wild sage. Three mile from the pass we came to the Pacific Springs where we found an express Post Office and had the privilege of sending letters to the States. We came on three miles to Pacific Creek. Found good grass and camped. Traveled ten miles.

June 29, Came 20 miles today over a barren country without grass or water. Camped on the Little Sandy. Found poor grass.

Last night it was decided by a vote of the company that we take the Salt Lake route and today we came to the fork of the road and took the Salt Lake road.

Sunday
June 30, Moved 5 miles to Big Sandy to find grass. Found good grass and lay up until Monday.

July 1, Last night one of our men, **Reuben Trowbridge**, was taken very sick with chill fever so that he was scarcely able to ride but we traveled 22 miles and camped on the Big Sandy and traveling made him no worse.

July 2, This morning we came to Green River. Found it very high and about 40 rods wide and a very rapid

current. Swam our cattle over. Had good luck.
Ferried our things over in a wagon box as we did over
the Platte. Got 5 wagons over today but it was a very
bad place to ferry as we had to wade in the water to
tow the board up along shore. **Charles Hale, E.M.
Blair** and several others were suddenly taken very
sick today.

July 3, The sick ones are better, all except one who
was taken last nigh very severely from the effects of
being in the water. We got the rest of our wagons all
safely over today. About 10:00 o'clock this afternoon
we moved down the river about 5 miles and camped
near Green River. Grass very poor.

July 4, It is a beautiful morning and we heard it
saluted with the discharge of firearms from the camps
around us and we answered them with a round from
our guns and a few cheers. One of our men, **A.
Walker**, is very sick and our starting is delayed until
10:00 o'clock on his account. When he appeared
much better, started and made 18 miles-15 without
water over barren, sandy, gravelly country. Camped
on Black Fork, a stream 6 rods and 3 feet deep.
Found good grass.

July 5, Today we passed Ham's Fork, a stream 3 rods
wide and 2 feet deep. Saw some Indians which were
the first we have seen for 500 miles. Saw a
Frenchman among them who had been there 19 years

trading among them; had a squaw for a wife, and said he enjoyed himself well. He told us that he had heard that the emigrants had killed some Indians to get away their horses and that the Indians intended to have revenge on some of the Whites-it made no difference who.

The news alarms some of our company and made them see the necessity of being on guard. Made 25 miles. Found good grass.

July 6, Today we moved 16 miles to a very rapid creek near Fort Bridger. Found good grass and concluded to stay all night. In the afternoon a Frenchman came to our wagons and wanted to sell us some beef. He had some Indian ponies to trade for cattle. Some of our boys talked of trading cattle but have not yet.

July 7, Our sick ones are getting better and we started about 1:00 o'clock P.M. Traveled about 8 miles over a high ridge. Could look back and see the snowy mountains at the south pass more than 100 miles distant. Today we passed Fort Bridger, or rather Bridger's trading post as there are no soldiers there. **Mr. Bridger** told us that there had been murders committed by the emigrants for no other reason thatn to get away the Indian's horses and he told us that we had better be on our guard. This afternoon we came up to a small company that were waiting for a larget force to come up as they though it unsafe to proceed alone. We joined with them and it increaases our company to 41 men. We camped near a stream of clear spring water.   Found good grass.

July 8, Last night about sundown we saw three Indians coming towards us on horseback at a gallop. They came up to us and one was a very smart Indian and could talk English. He appeared friendly and told us that the whites had killed 9 men and 20 women and children. He also told us that the Indians were gathering in large numbers in the neightborhood, but we have heard that **Mr. Bridger** is using his endeavors to keep them from shedding innocent blood. These are the Snake Indians. Are good warriors and well armed with good rifles.

Today we have passed over a very mountainous road but a good one most of the way. Those mountains are the dividing ridge between the water of the Colorado and the Salt Lake. Near the top of the mountains we passed a strong copperous spring.

We came 22 miles and camped near Sulphur Creek. Good water and good grass.

July 9, Today we made 21 miles over a very mountainous road. Crossed Bear River-a very rapid stream and a difficult crossing. Bear River is the place where the Indians were murdered, but we saw

no remains or sights on the road. We have now
passed by most of the Snake Indians and they have
not disturbed us.

We are getting into a grass country although very
mountainous, but our cattle have grass a-plenty and
most of them are doing well.

July 10, Today we have been traveling down a deep
revine with very high mountains on each side.
Crossed Echo Creek nearly 20 times and in some
places very difficult.

We made 20 miles and camped on red fork of Weber
River with grass around us 2 feet high and are within
40 miles of the city of Salt Lake.

July 11, Crossed Weber River without much trouble,
although it is a very rapid stream and about 3 feet
deep. Left the river in the afternoon and struck over
the mountains and had a difficult road but came 20
miles and camped on good grass.

Today we came over another mountain and down a
creek between high mountains and had a very bad
road. Came about 15 miles and learned that the city
is 13 miles further and it will take us another day to
get there. For the last week we have had very cold
nights and it has frozen ice 1/2" thick.

July 12, Today we came through a very deep revine
and a very bad road. Crossed a creek 19 or 20 times
in 6 miles. Turned over one wagon but injured
nothing very serious.

We struck the valley of Salt Lake 7 miles from the
city, on the southeast side. Moved up to the north
side of the City and camped, but had very poor grass.

Yesterday in the afternoon **A.S. Creamer**, one of our
company, accidently shot off his thumb but it is not
very painful and the doctor thinks it will grow on and
make a good thumb.

Sunday
July 14, All went to meeting to the Mormon Church.
Hear four sermons and one that was anything like
preaching. That was from a young man. Among the
rest was **Brigham Young**. His preaching consised of
bragging of his power and wisdom and of giving
orders to the Mormons with regard to selling wheat
and flour to emigrants. He told them they must have
25 cents per pound, and Monday morning we were
obliged to pay that for it and $8 to $10 per busel for
wheat. We were obliged to get our oxen shod on
Monday.

July 15, Some of teams started Monday night to get
better feed. 8 miles found good grass and we camped.

July 16, Teams moved 10 miles and waited for the teams behind.

July 17. Made 22 miles. Crossed Weber River and camped. Good feed and water.

July 18, Moved on about 8 miles and as the other teams have not yet come up we concluded to wait until they came up. Here I will take the liberty to give a short description of the valley of Salt Lke.

The valley is 150 miles long and 50 broad, and there are over valleys, which are settled, extending 200 or 300 miles south.

The city is laid out in wards and the wards are divided into lots and the lots are subdivided so that each citizen has 1 1/4 acres. There are 20 wards and covers a space of about 2000 acres. The land is tolerable good but not equal to Illinois, but they raise first rate wheat, but a poor corn country. The Mormons are obliged to irrigate their land for there is no rain here in the summer and very little in the winter. The city is well situated near the mountain on a descending slope of land and the water is carried into every part of the city and all through every man's field. The water is good and a great plenty of it. There is but a small part of the valley that is good for cultivation, as it is covered in many places with water and much swampy land.

I have been told that there are 20,000 inhabitants in the valley.

The Mormons believe everything that **Brigham Young** says and will do anything that he tells them to. Also, that he is an inspired Prophet and everything he says is revealed to him.

July 19, The rest of the teams came up last night and today we moved 25 miles over a good road with high mountains on our right whose tops are covered with snow and the valley and lake on our left. In one place we passed near the Salt Lake and a company of us took the liberty to bathe in its water. Since we left the city we have passed many hot springs, some salt springs and an abundance of first rate cold spring water. In one place we passed one hot spring and one cold one not more than 30 feet apart.

July 20, Today we moved up to Bear River, crossed it on a ferry boat - paid $5.00 ferrage per wagon. Had good luck. 2 miles from the river crossed a creek on a bridge one rod wide and paid one dollar toll. Made 15 miles and camped by a small creek. Good grass.

July 21, Left the Salt Lake Valley and struck west among the mountains. Had good roads. Made 15 miles. Camped near several springs of water but it is all brackish and hardly fit to drink.

July 22, The country begins to look barren and grass is getting scarce. Passed one small creek of good water which ran about 80 rods on top ofthe ground and then sank. Came 20 miles and camped on a creek 8 feet wide and 6 feet deep. Found a small patch of good grass.

July 23, Traveled all day over a level barren flat. Found a little water at noon but no grass. Camped on the side of the mountain after having filled our water cage at a small spring. Found tolerable grass 1 1/2 miles from the spring. Distance 20 miles.

July 24, Traveled most of the day on the bench of a mountain. Crossed several creeks. Had a good road but no grass. Made 10 miles. Camped on Cassus Creek and found good grass at night. Cassus Creek and all the rest of the creeks and springs that we have passed for the last two days sink after running a few miles on top of the ground.

July 25, Today we moved up the creek ten miles. Found good grass and camped. As we are now within 5 miles of the junction of this road with the Fort Hill road we expect short feed when we get there and think it best to give our teams a chance before reaching the great crowd that is on the other road.

July 26, Started early this morning and struck off through the mountains. Passed the celebrated steeple

rocks which are very high with a true taper to the top.
These rocks are near the junction of the two roads.
This afternoon we have passed over a high ridge of
mountains and some very bad road. We camped on
Goose Creek. Found better grass than we expected.
Made 21 miles. Since we came on the Fort Hall road
we have passed 6 new made graves, and heard that is
has been very sickly on that road.

Last night we had a very hard shower and some hail.
There has been showers all around us for the last few
days, which is uncommon in this country.

July 27, Followed up Goose Creek 15 miles. There is
good grass all the way. Filled our water cage and left
the creek then came 6 miles into the mountains over a
hilly rough road and camped. Found no grass nor
water for our cattle. Two men have just died, one on
each side of us just a few rods distance; one of the
cholera and one of the consumption. It seems to be
quite sicly on the road.

We have heard from the emigaration behind us and
are told thousands of emigrants have died with the
cholera and thousands of teams have gone back to the
States.

I think that there will be a great deal of suffering on
the road not only from sickness but for want of
provisions, for hundreds are already getting out of

breadstuff and $1.00 per pound has been offered for flour.   Bacon has been thrown away in great profusion 200 miles back but now it sells for 25 cents per pound.

We have seen large numbers of dead cattle and horses today. Counted 32 head which is more than we saw on the whole of Salt Lake road.

July 28, Left our camping place before sunrise. Came 10 miles to Thousand Spring Valley. Expected to find grass but it was all gnawed close to the ground, but by moving about 4 miles found some but very poor. There are numerous springs and natural wells in this valley 6 miles further brought us to another valley. Found poor water and but tolerable grass. Whole distance today 20 miles.

July 29, Today we rolled up the valley. Passed large quantities of good grass but left the creek and the grass in the afternoon expecting to come to another creek but have been deceived by the guide which we bought in Salt Lake. It is not correct as to distance. We passed some hot springs nearly at the boiling point. Came 20 miles and camped about 1 mile from the road. Found a small patch of grass-some springs of water.

July 30, Left the valley this morning and came through a gap in the mountains-rather hilly but most of the day had a first rate road. Last night **Charles Sawyer** lost an ox which is the first the company has lost since we left the Missouri.

Last night the Indians stole 16 horses from two different companies camped within 10 or 12 miles of us.

We are now camped in a beautiful valley with a very high mountain a few miles to the south of us whose top is covered with snow. Plenty of good grass in the valley and a good sping of water near us. Distance today 22 miles.

July 31, Last night our cattle got poisoned with some poisoned grass or weeds and have been sick ever since. We have doctored them thoroughly but we fear we shall lose some of them.

We rolled down the valley over a beautiful road 15 miles with good grass on each side of us all the way. We passed a singular creek where we crossed it it was perfectly dry. A few miles down we found the water 7 feet deep, about 1 rod wide and with a strong current, 3 miles further it sank entirely and was perfectly dry.

We are now camped on the Humbolt or Marys river. It is a clear stream one rod wide and two feet deep.

August 1, Last night was very cold and it froze ice as thick as a window glass. Our cattle are getting better. We rolled 22 miles over a good road down Marys river.

This afternoon 5 of our men went a-hunting and saw a large lot of Indians who appeared very wild and hostile and they thought best to let them alone.

August 2, This morning a man was found by the side of the road in the last agonies of death and died in a few minutes. There was nothing about him by which we could discover his name of the company to which he belonged. We buried him as decently as circumstances would permit.

Last night we came to the Packer's road which came across the desert from Salt Lake. Some of the Packer's had just come through who started from Salt Lake about the same time we did. They say it is a hard cutoff and have traveled around the mountains farther than we have. They have come across the 75 mile desert which almost killed their horses. They told us that they saw many horses in the hands of Indians which they had stolen from the emigrants.

We made 22 miles over a good road.

August 3, Last night two oxen were shot by the
Indians with arrows. One belonged to **Mr. Murray**
who is traveling in our company.

The Indians are very troublesome here and have stolen
many horses here within a few days.

Today we have traveled over a rough road. Crossed
the river 4 times. Made 16 miles. Found good grass.

August 4, Today the road turned over the mountains.
Had quite a rough road. Struck the river again in
about 17 miles. Whole distance today 21 miles. We
found good grass across the river.

August 5, Rolled out this morning at sunrise and
traveled 24 miles. A portion of the road was over a
rough hilly country and the whole distance was very
dusty and disagreeable traveling. Found good grass
but poor water.

August 6, Made 22 miles today. Had a good road
most of the way. A great protion of the road has been
over saleratus ground. It is crusted over in many
places 1/2" thick. Camped without any good water
but had good grass about 2 miles from the river.

August 7, Rolled on 24 miles today over level road
down the river at a distance 2 or 3 miles from it over a

barren clayish soil destitiute of grass, but found good grass at night by turning a mile off the road.

After we had camped, an old Mormon came to our camp and wanted his supper. He had just come from California. We gave him his supper and got some informaiton from him of the road ahead and the desert.

August 8, The road has been good today except a short distance over rocky bluffs.   Some of the lowland is covered with salt 1/2' deep. came 22 miles and camped near the river. Found good grass. the water is very muddy. The river here is 6 or 8 feet deep.

August 9, Our road today has been over barren sandy land and very heavy wheeling. The old road goes near the river but the water is so high and the flats so miry that it is impossible to travel across the flats in many places. There is a slough that runs nearly the whole length of the river and is very miry and it is difficult getting to the grass but we have generally managed to get it some way. Made 21 miles today.

August 10, This morning we came to the last crossing of the Humbolt River.   It is 10 or 12 feet deep. We crossed our things in a wagon box. Hauled some wagons through the stream with ropes. Turned some of our wagons over in the river but we got them out without injury and were detained but 3 hours.

We traveled over a heavy sandy road until 9:00
o'clock when we arrived at the river but found no
grass. Made 20 miles.

August 11, In the morning we found some grass
across the river and with some difficulty we got our
cattle across to it but the ground was very miry and
some of our cattle got stuck in the mud.

As we expected an introduction to the desert, we think
it necessary to cut some grass to take along with us.
In order to get it we were oblliged to swim across the
river and cut it and then had to draw it across with
ropes.

Started about 1:00 o'clock and drove 10 miles and
found grass across the river.

August 12, Our road today has been over a very
dusty road and has been very hard on the teams. We
have driven 23 miles without any grass except what
we brought with us.

August 13,   This morning we drove 5 miles to the
river. Found but very little grass and that was across
the river and it was very miry-dangerous for cattle.
Had to haul some of our cattle out with ropes. Left
the river at 1:00 o'clock and drove 18 miles and

expected to find grass but all that we found was cut
and hauled up from the great meadow for sale at 20
cents a handful of about 10 lbs.   We bought some for
our cattle and camped.

August 14, We drove down the river 6 miles and
camped by the side of an inexhaustible meadow of
grass and canes. Here we found thousands of people
laying up recruiting their cattle and cutting grass and
drying it to last them across the desert. We went at it
like the rest and cut some grass but we had a
disagreeable job of it for the grass grows in the water
from one to two feet deep and we have to carry it on
our backs through the water to the river and then haul
it across in a wagon box and then spread it out to dry
The river here is 4 rods wide and 10 to 12 feet deep.

August 15., Today we have finished cutting and
drying our grass and have been making preparations
for crossing the desert.

For the last few days we passed large quantities of
dead cattle and horses and some that were yet alive
and were left to suffer on the sandy barren plains. I
should think we have passed, some days, 100 head of
dead stock in a day.

The cattle and horses are not the only sufferers on the
road to California for many people are getting out of
provisions. There are some inquiring for provisions

almost constantly; some say they have been without bread for severals days. Many cattle have been killed on the road to get meat to subsist on. I think that one half of the emigrants now on the road are entirely out of bread stuff. Some have had a little to sell and flour has sold for $2.00 per pound.

Thousands of dollars worth of property has been destroyed & thrown away. It consists of wagons (or the iron of wagons as the wood work is burned up), clothing, guns, harnesses, chains, etc.   One of the men counted 15 gun barrels at one old encampment.

August 16, We left our encampment this morning and rolled on 20 miles. Our cattle got something that poisoned them and some of them have been quite sick. We camped by the side of a lake without a particle of vegetation near us.

August 17, This morning we left what is called the sink of the Humbolt River, but as there was much more water in the river this year than usual, some of it runs 10 miles further before it all sinks, and we came very unexpectedly to a part of the river which was 3 feet deep and we had to unload our wagons and carry our things across the stream on our backs. Here we left the last water before crossing the desert, which is 40 miles.

We traveled all night and our teams stood it first rate
for we had grass and water for our cattle which we
brought with us. This stretch is 65 miles without
grass and without water.   Many others were not as
fortunate as we were crossing this desert for some
people have lost all their teams and have thrown their
wagons and most of their effects away. All the
property we have seen destroyed and all the dead
stock we have seen on the whole trip is nothing
compared with what we have seen on this desert. I
should think we have passed a thousand head of dead
stock and half as many wagons in the last 10 miles of
the desert.

August 18, Early this morning we passed some men
who had haulded water from Carson's River and were
selling it at $1.00 per gallon and some at $1.00 per
gill and other things in proportion.

We came down to Carson's River about 2 miles and
camped but found very poor grass. The distance we
have made the last two days is about 50 miles.

August 19, This morning we moved up the river
about 2 miles for grass. Found it better but rather
short. Stayed until 4:00 o'clock P.M> and then we
moved up the river 3 miles and from there we struck
across a sandy desert of 15 miles. Had beautiful
moonlight. Came to the river about 1:00 o'clock A.M.
Found good grass and camped.

There are a number of trading establishments where we first struck this river carried on by men from California. They have provisons to sell and they buy up the poor cattle that are tired out and broken down for about from $3.00 to $10.00 each, intending to recruit them and take them over to California.

August 20, We let our cattle rest until 2:00 o'clock and then moved on across a very sandy desert. Had very heavy wheeling all the way. Distance across 12 miles. Came to the river. Found good grass and camped.

August 21, Rolled up the river today 25 miles. Good road and good grass most of the way. Found tolerable grass at night. This river is about 6 rods wide and 3 feet deep and is clear and good water which is quite a rarity. There is some cotton wood timber scattered along this river and plenty of willow brush.

August 22, This morning we crossed the river and traveled over a rough hilly road. Came to the river in 10 miles. Left the river again in the afternood and came to the river again after traveling 8 miles over a sandy road. Found an abundance of the very best of grass. (18 miles) There are miners prospecting and digging on this river but can't tell how much gold they are getting.

We have met several companies of men from the west
side of the mountains with their gold washers and
mining tools going down to work on Carson's river.
We have passed two trading posts today. They sell
flour at $1.50 per pound. sugar, dried apples and
pork at that price.

August 23, Rolled up the valley 16 miles over a good
road and found an abundance of grass all the way.
Met a caravan of mules packed with flour from
Sacramento going down the river to sell to the
emigrants who are suffering for it but few have money
to buy it at such high prices.

We are now at the foot of the Sierra Nevada
mountains. Their sides are covered with pine timber
and the tops with snow.

August 24, We have moved along the valley near the
foot of the mountains 10 miles. Stopped to recruit our
cattle before entering the mountains. Intending to roll
up the Sierra Nevada tomorrow.

August 25, This morning myself and others left the
teams to go on to the mines ahead. Took a blanket
coat and 2 day's provisions and after a walk of about
4 miles we entered a deep canyon with mountains on
each side 4,000 to 5,000 feet high and through the
worst road I ever saw over tremendous rocks, steep
and crooked - almost impossible for a wagon to get

through. These mountains and valley are covered with pine timber; some trees of a very large size 8 feet in diameter. This is the first timber of any note that we have seen since we left Iowa. There was some in the mountains around Salt Lake.

We stopped at noon at Kenyon Valley under the shade of a balsam tree and got a cup of coffee and some dinner, and after resting an hour we started and traveled 12 miles up the valley where the road is quite decent and there is some grass along the valley. Passed a beautiful lake this afternoon called Red Lake.

We camped in a deep valley surrounded with high mountains whose tops are covered with snow. We are now taking our comfort by the side of a large fire made of pine logs. Distance today 24 miles.

August 26, Started this morning up the mountain. About 3/4 of a mile over a very steep and rocky road brought us to the top of the first mountain, then we descended into a deep valley where there is a beautiful lake and green grass. We left this valley and began to ascend another mountain. 5 miles brought us to the top of the noted Sierra Nevada, or snowy mountain. Here we passed over many snow banks some of which appeared to be 50 feet deep.

The summit of this mountain at this place is 8,000 feet high but in some places it is said to be 16,000 feet above the level of the sea. Here the air is cold and chilly. Stopped on the top of the mountain and took dinner and refreshed ourselves with a drink of cool water that issued out of a rock.

In the afternoon we came to a path which we thought was a cutoff and followed it but it led us off into the mountains several miles from the road and at last the path vanishes, and some of us took one course and some another and I soon found myself traveling over mountains of solid granite rocks. I took my course and about 10 miles travel brought me to the camp of 3 men within half a mile of the road. Most of the distance which I have traveled since I left the road has been over granite rocks and through almost impenetrable thickets which are a resort for the Grizzly bear. The whole day's travel today had been through a region of snow.I camped with the three men above alluded to. The distance today I should think is 25 miles.

August 27, I started this moring at 6:00 o'clock and traveled all day on the ridge of mountains with deep valleys on each side. The road is getting better and is through heavy pine timber, some of the most beautiful that I ever saw. There are traders all along the road selling flour at from 40 cents to 50 cents per pound, beef 30 cents, pork 50 cents, potatoes 40 cents per lb.

I have traveled 35 miles today and camped 1/2 mile off the road in the thick brush near a spring. The men that I left yesterday I have not seen yet. I think they are behind.

August 28, Ten miles further brought me down off the ridge of mountains into Pleasant Valley. Stopped at Pleasant Valley and got dinner. Here the road is good but no grass. Ten miles further brought me to Weaverville. a temporary stopping place for the emigrant. This place is in the vicinity of the gold mines and some stop here to dig for gold.

Weaverville is 55 miles from Sacramento City. Flour is selling here for 15 cents to 20 cents per lb. pork 30 cents, beef 25 cents.

August 29, Went over the mountains 3 miles to Placerville. Found Mr. Hopkins who left the team one week before I did. He was driving teams at $2.00 per day. There are a great many digging gold here but they are scarcely making their board, but there are a few that are doing well. Board is worth $3.00 per day and $15.00 per week.

The whole distance from the Missiour River to Sacramento City is 1927 miles. Distance from Salt Lake 896 miles.

Caleb Trowbridge

Caleb Trowbridge made his home in his native town (New Haven, Connecticut) and turned to the sea for an occupation. becoming a captain of a vessel at an early age.

At the outbreak of the Revolution he had become a well-known man in his profession. The Second Company, Governor's Foot Guard, had been organized shortly before the Lexington alarm and it volunteered for service, being out twenty-eight days. He was commissioned captain of this company, succeeding **Benedict Arnold** (then appointed a colonel) May 1, 1775.

Soon after he received a captain's commission he returned to New Haven, and in a few days raised a fine company of volunteers. He employed a man named **Fitzgerald** to teach them the manual exercise, and they met for that purpose in **Captain Trowbridge's** parlor, which for a time was changed into a drill-room.

He served until his discharge December 10. He re-entered the service the following year and served with the 1st Regiment of Continentals under **General Wooster** at the siege of Boston.

He was commissioned on January 1, 1776, captain in **Jedediah Huntington's** regiment, the 17th Continentals, after the siege of Boston and marched under **Washington** to New York.

He was ordered to the Brooklyn front and took part in the battle of Long Island, August 27, 1776, and near Greenwood cemetery he and most of his company were surrounded by the enemy and taken prisoner.

Captain Trowbridge's term of service expired December 31, 1776, but "he was a prisoner nearly two years", a part of the time on Long Island, and the remainder in the old sugar house on Liberty street, which was removed but a few years ago.

It was his unwillingness to yield to the wishes of his captors that caused him to be detained so long a prisoner, as an officer of equal rank was frequently offered in exchange. The British demanded that he should not again take up arms against them, a consideration to which he would not agreed. On the contrary, he told them that as soon as he should get his liberty, he would beat them again".

His imprisonment was much easier than it would have been had not his wife sold her plate, and found means to forward him the money to Long Island, with which he purchased many privileges that were denied to other prisoners. Upon his release he returned to New

Haven, and after waiting some time for a major's commission, which had been promised him, he became impatient, repaired to Boston, and taking out letters of marque, commenced a warrior's life upon the sea.

After remaining in this calling awhile, he again returned to New Haven. A company of citizens had fitted out a vessel for the West Indies, which was upon the point of sailing when the British cruisers made their appearance. The vessel was taken above the bridge, and shot fired at her, in order to sink her, and thereby prevent her falling into the enemy's hands, when, by some accident, she took fire and burnt to the water's edge. The hull was soon after raised, built into a brig, and fitted out for a trading voyage to Holland, and **Captain Trowbridge** put in command. She was well armed, and took several prizes. She made two voyages to Amsterdam in the most exciting period in the war, when the ocean was covered with British cruisers, in search of French, Spanish, Dutch and American vessels. The name of this little vessel was The Fire Brand, from the circumstance of her having been built from a burned hull."

The house of **Captain Trowbridge**, on the corner of Water and Meadow streets, did not fare as well at the time of the British invasion of New haven as did that of his cousin **Rutherford**. It was furnished with unusual elegance for those days, and was replete with conveniences and luxuries, and the cellar was stored with choice wines and liquors. The enemy, on learning that the owner was the commander of a war vessel cruising against British commerce, sacked his house, and brought his fine furniture out to the street and burned it. Long afterward when the house was undergoing repairs, bullets were found in the ceiling and the wainscoting which had been fired into the building by the British."

The following anecdote of **Captain Trowbridge** strongly illustrates his firmness and decision of character:--

"Before the war **Trowbridge** and **Arnold** had some account together, the settlement of which led to a dispute. They parted, **Arnold** saying, ' You meet me tomorrow morning at – o'clock (naming the hour), and we will settle it,' **Mr. Trowbridge** supposed him to be joking, and thought no more of it. Early the next morning he was called from his bed by two gentlemen, who requested to see him on particular business, and when informed that **Arnold** had repaired to the spot designated by him the day previous, he was much surprised, but expressed his determination to meet. Nor were entreaties to dissuade him from it of any avail. Upon repairing to the swamp, just west of the present residence of **Dr. Totten**, he found **Arnold** waiting for him. He advanced towards him, when **Arnold** drew two pistols, and told him to choose one of them. He was much surprised, but not frightened, and without giving time to **Arnold** to guard himself, rushed upon him and wrenched both pistols from him, throwing them into the creek, and told him to go home; an order which he was not long in performing."

Captain Trowbridge was elected a member of Hiram Lodge No. 1, F. and A.M,. Of New Haven in 1767.

Taken from **Trowbridge** Genealogy Pg 64 and 65

Artemas Ward

October 28 1800: Revolutionary War Commander **Artemas Ward** Dies

On This Day......in 1800, the man who commanded the ragtag American force that chased the British Regulars back to Boston following the battles of Lexington and Concord died at home in Shrewsbury, Massachusetts. Trusted and admired by the volunteer militiamen who made up the first American army, General **Artemas Ward** was severely criticized by **George Washington**, who assumed command of the Continental Army in July 1775. Accustomed to serving with professional officers, **Washington** and his fellow Virginians dismissed **Ward** as "a fat old church warden." **Washington** was also appalled by the lax discipline among **Ward**'s New England soldiers. After two years, **Artemas Ward** resigned and returned home to Shrewsbury. The Massachusetts general faded from national memory and from the history books.

Background

Artemas Ward at mid-life was not an impressive looking fellow; his biographer described him as "a man of medium height; . . . too stout for his forty-seven years, and . . . showing the effects of . . . illness." He had neither great wealth nor high social position. But in the spring of 1775, as crisis loomed in Massachusetts, the colony's Committee of Safety chose **Ward** to be the Commander-in-Chief of the "Grand American Army," as the newspapers referred to the collection of local militia units that were preparing for war.

The revolutionary leaders trusted **Ward**'s judgment. He was a Puritan, a patriot, and a man "fully convinced that 'those of Massachusetts were the Chosen People.'" He had proved his mettle through 24 years of public and military service. More important, **Ward** had the trust, respect, and affection of the militiamen, and they were willing to follow him. In the spring and summer of 1775, **Ward**'s ability to command their loyalty would prove critical.

Artemas Ward was born and grew up in the
Worcester County town of Shrewsbury, which his
parents, both of old Puritan stock, had helped found.
In 1748, at the age of 20, he graduated from Harvard
and took a position teaching school in Groton. There
he met his future wife, **Sarah Trowbridge**. After their
marriage in 1750, the couple settled in Shrewsbury.
While his wife bore eight children, **Ward** kept a farm
and a busy general store. He was elected to numerous
offices, including representative to the General Court
in Boston.

In 1758 **Ward** was commissioned as a major in a
provincial regiment raised for the French and Indian
War. Meritorious service earned him promotion to
lieutenant-colonel, but the difficult campaign in the
Adirondacks ruined his health. He never fully
regained his strength.

His reputation, however, did not suffer. On his return
to Shrewsbury, he was appointed colonel of his militia
regiment, and in 1762, a judge of the Court of
Common Pleas. For the next decade, he distinguished
himself with his dogged opposition to royal authority,
drawing the wrath of crown officials and the
admiration of patriots.

In the fall of 1774, as British troops occupied Boston
and the sense of impending hostilities grew, the
Massachusetts Provincial Congress ordered each town

to train a militia. By February of 1775, as tensions increased, it was clear that the local militia units could no longer report only to their own officers. They would need a general commander. **Artemas Ward** got the job.

When fighting broke out on April 19th, **Ward** lay sick at home in Shrewsbury with a painful attack of "bladder stones." The next morning, despite his condition, he rode 35 miles to Cambridge to take command of the various militia that had chased the British Regulars back to Boston.

Ward maintained the siege of Boston in its initial months and fortified the patriot position by taking the strategic high point of Bunker Hill.

Ward faced formidable challenges. Not only was he confronting the world's most powerful army, but he was doing so with a force of volunteers who had agreed only to turn out for a single battle. Once the British had been driven back to Boston, many militiamen wanted to return to their farms. They had not enlisted, and had little enthusiasm for camp life, especially given the rough and unhygienic conditions of their impromptu camp at Cambridge.

Ward had the daunting task of creating an army. He appealed for volunteers to become the first enlistees. Men from Massachusetts, New Hampshire,

Connecticut, and Rhode Island began to fill the ranks. Critics complained that **Ward** was a lax disciplinarian and that his "Grand American Army" was anything but grand. But **Artemas Ward** understood his volunteer Yankee soldiers. He knew that they would not tolerate, and that he had no legal authority to impose, strict discipline. He had to lead by consensus and mutual respect, for, as one patriot wrote to **Samuel Adams**, "our soldiers will not be brought to obey any person of whom they do not themselves entertain a high opinion." **Ward**'s deft management helped his raw recruits hold the siege.

On June 17th, the Continental Congress in Philadelphia debated who should be appointed supreme commander of the American forces. **John Adams** reported that "the greatest number" wanted the job to go to **Ward**. However, an overriding concern was to persuade delegates from the South that this was not just New England's war. The Congress chose **George Washington** of Virginia and made **Ward** his second in command.

Two weeks later, **Washington** arrived in Cambridge; he immediately began criticizing **Ward** publicly and in writing. **Artemas Ward** was deeply offended, and relations between the two men never improved.

Two years later, suffering from ill health, **Ward** resigned his position and returned to Shrewsbury. He served for the next 20 years as representative to the Continental, First, and Second Congresses.

After his death in 1800, **Ward** faded into obscurity. Historians remembered him mostly as the inept commander portrayed by **Washington** or not at all. Even the central Massachusetts town named in his honor eventually changed its name to "Auburn." A great-grandson donated **Ward**'s Shrewsbury home and $5,000,000 to Harvard University on the condition that the university work to restore the general's reputation. Recently, graduate students have begun to use the home and its collections as a scholarly resource to learn more about the life and times of the nation's first military commander-in-chief.

Catherine McClish

One of the stories that I haven't quite proven but sounds logical is concerning my Great Great grandmother **Catherine McClish**.

I had heard that there was a possibility that she might have been "raped" by an Indian and became pregnant with the child **David McClish** (my great grandfather). I think the story might have been that she was captured by Indians (as there were major tribes in the area) and may have married into the tribe and became pregnant. When the US government required the Indians to give up their white captives, she might have been one of them. Not wanting to accept the possibility that she willingly became pregnant with an Indian, the story was that she was raped.

I have done a lot of research on the nature of the American Indian and found the act of rape was considered to be a violation of their laws and was dealt with usually by banning the guilty one from the tribe. In effect "outcasting". If that were the case and **Catherine** was raped, then the guilty one would have been banished. If she married and it was not rape it is possible that when the government required the return of the white prisoners, the Indians released her and she was returned to her family.

Catherine Walters and Robert McClish

Now, in this case it is possible that when she married **Samuel Croy**, he did not want to accept a "half breed" and that was the reason that **David** was raised by his grandfather and grandmother **(Robert** and **Catherine Walters McClish)**. It is obvious that **Catherine** had limited time with her son until after her divorce from **Samuel**, so that is a possibility.

This is not to blame **Samuel**, as it was a custom of the day for people to look down on the Indians. This was due to misunderstanding of this race.   So far, I admit I have no proof of all this, only a research into the nature of the American Indian. BUT it does make for some speculation and I welcome anyone who has more information on this to contact me and educate me on what happened.

John Adams

Born in a different time and place, **John Adams**
might have lived a contented life as a country lawyer
and farmer. Instead, he was catapulted to greatness as
a revolutionary, diplomat, and nation builder.
Learned, thoughtful, and deeply principled, he was by
nature a philosopher, yet events forced him to play the
role of a pragmatic politician.

Adams was born on a farm in Braintree,
Massachusetts, a quiet village just south of Boston.
He always loved the farm and farming, but his
intellectual gifts were unmistakable. His father
decided that his son should be educated for the
ministry. He attended the town schools, was tutored
in Latin, and entered Harvard in 1751.

John Adams's four years at Harvard opened new worlds to him and awakened a passion for science, debate, and oration. He was soon more interested in a career as a physician, lawyer, or government official than a clergyman. After graduation, he served an apprenticeship with a Worcester lawyer by the name of **Edmund Trowbridge**, before being admitted to the bar.

In 1758, **Adams** returned home to Braintree and opened a law office. Like other country lawyers in colonial Massachusetts, he went to Boston often on legal business. He acquired a circle of friends — including his distant cousin **Sam Adams** — who were concerned with, and increasingly angered by, the way the British Parliament treated the colonies. **Adams** began to articulate his ideas on the nature of freedom and the universal rights of men. In a series of anonymous articles for the Boston Gazette, he set forth the philosophical, legal, and religious justifications for protesting the oppressive acts of Parliament. His carefully reasoned arguments helped lay the intellectual groundwork for colonial resistance.

Adams's frequent trips to Boston took him past the Weymouth home of **Rev. William Smith**. In 1759, he first met the middle of **Smith**'s three daughters, 15-year-old **Abigail**. They were married after a five-year courtship. While others might find **John Adams** blunt, irascible, and sometimes thin-skinned,

Abigail Smith fell in love with his wit, integrity, and strength of character; in her eyes, he was nothing less than "a giant of great heart." He found her intelligent, good-natured, and steady. Both were strong-minded. As one biographer put it, **John Adams's** marriage "was the most important decision of [his] life." The devoted couple would support and nurture each other for the next 63 years — many of them spent apart.

In 1765, news reached America that Parliament had passed the Stamp Act, a measure **Adams** referred to as "the enormous engine fabricated by the British Parliament for battering down all the rights and liberties of America." An outraged **Adams** wrote the official protest for Braintree. "We have always understood it to be a grand and fundamental principle of the [English] constitution that no freeman should be subject to any tax to which he has not given his own consent." In a matter of weeks, more than 40 towns had adopted the "Braintree Instructions."

As respect for his legal and political skills grew, **Adams** relocated his household and law practice to Boston, where he became the city's busiest attorney. (The family would move back to the relative safety of Braintree in 1774.)

John Adams's distaste for royal authority was well known, but he was an independent thinker with a deep fear of "mob rule." When British soldiers were charged with murder in the Boston Massacre, he viewed the incident as the result of unlawful behavior by an unruly crowd and volunteered to represent the hated "Lobsterbacks." Pro-independence newspapers were quick to attack his position, but he won acquittals for the soldiers and established himself as a man of principle who would not be swayed by public opinion.

During the years leading up to the Revolution, **Adams** became committed to the cause of independence. As one of five Massachusetts delegates to the First Continental Congress in Philadelphia, he insisted that the colonies needed to take decisive action to sever ties with Britain. While other delegates hesitated, he led the movement to declare independence.

When the declaration finally came, he wrote prophetically to his beloved **Abigail**, "The day will be celebrated by succeeding generations as the great anniversary festival. It ought to be commemorated as the Day of Deliverance by solemn acts of devotion to God Almighty. It ought to be solemnized with pomp and parade, with shows, games, sports, guns, bells, bonfires, and illuminations from one end of this continent to the other from this time forward and forever more."

As **George Washington** assumed command of the
Continental Army, **Adams** was appointed to the
Board of War and given the difficult task of equipping
the troops. In 1777, Congress decided he was needed
in Europe; he sailed for France hoping to gain
diplomatic and material support for the new nation.

He had only been home a few months when Congress
sent him back to Europe to negotiate a peace treaty
with Great Britain. At the end of war, he was named
the first ambassador to England. Back at home, Shays'
Rebellion had bolstered support in the Constitutional
Convention for the strong central government **Adams**
favored. He returned to the United States in 1788, just
in time to see the new constitution ratified. Within a
year, he was elected the nation's first vice president,
and on April 13, 1789, he departed for the capital,
then in New York.

Although **Adams** called the vice presidency "the most
insignificant office that ever the invention of man
contrived," he held it for two terms. In the strife-filled
years of early nation-building, he was fiercely
independent; he decried and steered clear of the
growing partisanship that he feared would destroy the
fragile new republic.

Adams was elected the second president of the United
States and served from 1797 to 1801. While he
succeeded in keeping the country out of a looming

war with France, his popularity and reputation suffered from his support for the harsh Alien and Sedition Acts. Ultimately, he lost his bid for reelection because he refused, on principle, to embrace partisan politics.

The world watched in awe as **Adams** transferred power to **Thomas Jefferson**, once his ally and friend, now his opponent — a powerful demonstration of the democratic system both men had helped to create. **John Adams** returned to Massachusetts, where he lived for another 25 years.

Sources
Founding Brothers: The Revolutionary Generation, by **Joseph Ellis** (Knopf, 2000).

John Adams, by **David McCullough** (Simon and Schuster, 2001).

Alma Albertha Glines

I start this story with grandma's obit because it shows only a small part of her life. In some ways this lady was bigger than life. I was one of the fortunate... I got to know her. She died when I was only 3 ½ years old but she left an impact on my life that cannot be ignored. So after you read her obit... then follow me in the stories I know of my great grandmother.

Mrs. **Alma Alberta Solomon**, 85, for many years active in the work of the Salvation Army in New Castle, died Tuesday in the Henry County hospital after a week's illness. Her home was at 2422 State St.

Mrs. Solomon had been a worker in the Salvation Army here for 35 years; she had been a resident of this county for 64 years.

Surviving are two sons, **Lawrence** of New Castle and **Ernest** of New Orleans; 17 grandchildren and 21 great grandchildren.

Funeral services will be held Friday at 2 p.m. in the Salvation Army chapel. **Capt. Ellis** of Shelbyville, formerly of the Salvation Army in New Castle, will conduct rites. Burial will be in Hillsboro cemetery.

She was born 25 September 1866 in Randolph County, Indiana to **Isaac M. Glines** and **Margaret Cornelia Seagrave**. Her mother died when **Bertha** (as she was called) was just 2 years old. I believe this might have been part of the reason that she took my dad (**William Everett McClish**) to raise when his mother (her daughter **Olive Alice Solomon)** died. Dad was just 18 months old.

Bertha was no stranger to trials in her life. Her father remarried to **Sarah Ann Bailey** in 1870. From family stories, I am told that **Sarah** was the kind of mother that treated all the children as her own. **Sarah** and **Isaac** did have one child together, unfortunately he died as an infant.

On one occasion Grandma and my sister **Alice Ann** were walking and **Alice** spotted a homeless man on the street. She made some kind of bad remark and Grandma replied "there is something beautiful about that man. You go and find out what it is!" **Alice** had to cross the street and find out something about the man that was beautiful. She ran over and quickly looked at the man, then ran back and said "He has beautiful eyes." That satisfied grandma.

Grandma saw beauty in everything. You never heard
her say a bad thing about anything or anyone. I
wondered about this in years later, but thought it was
just Grandma. Recently, I found something that
explains a lot about her.

Grandma Solomon was a member of the Salvation
Army. She not only was a "member", she was an
"officer". I found that when she joined the Salvation
Army movement, she took some pretty specific vows.
This is a partial list of those vows:
1. She declared her full determination boldly, to show
herself a Soldier of Jesus Christ in all places and
companies, no mater what she may have to suffer, do,
or lose, by doing so.
2. She would abstain from the use of all intoxicating
liquors and from habitual use of drugs except those
ordered for her by a doctor.
3. She would abstain from the use of all low and
profane language, or from the taking of the name of
God in vane. She would abstain from taking part in
any unclean conversation or the reading of any
obscene book or paper at any time, in any company or
in any place.
4. She declared that she would never treat any
woman, child, or other person, whose life, comfort, or
happiness may be placed within her power, in any
oppressive, cruel, or cowardly manner, but that she
would protect such from evil and danger so far as she
could.

There is more, but these few give you an insite into this wonderful woman. She took my dad, when he was just eighteen month old, to raise. He was sickly but she felt it her responsibility to do so. She did not approve of my mother and father living together and not married but she did not turn her back on us either. Grandma lived what she preached.

One of my favorite stories of grandma was a Christmas story. She would go out and collect money for the poor as she felt it her responsibility to do so. In New Castle there was a "pool hall". Now to grandma, playing pool was a sin... so she went into the pool hall, she had decided that she would collect money from the people there, BUT when she got there and as she started to collect money, she looked around and low and behold what did she see....??? Her sons playing pool...she walked up to them and stated "If you have money to play pool, you have money for the poor." She made them give up their money....right then and there. That was grandma. This story was told to me by **Jim Solomon** (1919-2003) whose father **Frank Solomon (George Franklin Solomon** 1890-1951)** was one of the sons that was caught "playing pool".

Her life was her legacy. She left an impression on everyone she met. My only regret is that I did not get to spend more time with her. She was and is, my hero.

Back row: **Frank and Ada Solomon**
Middle row **Fielding Bailey Solomon, Alma Albertha Solomon** and **Ernie Solomon**
Front Row: **Anna Solomon**

Fragments

The following is of the early history of the **McClish** family as told by **Rob Bale**. **Rob** was one of the early investigators of our **McClish** history and one who contributed much to our stories. I am including his emails to me so that you can get an idea of our early history.

zongker-myers regina, dau of **Fredk-Barbara**, sister to **Jacob Myers** (1821-1884) aunt to **Eliza Ann McClish**

The first born of **Joseph Zangker** and **Anna Marie Roth** was **Joseph Martin** or **Joseph Zongker II.**

Joseph Martin was born April 1818 in Switzerland before the family came to the United States in 1818. The first place they were after arriving was in Pennsylvania. After entering through Philadelphia they first settled in Elizabethtown. perhaps in Lancaster County.

While in Seneca County we find **Joseph Martin** marrying **Regina Meyers** of Pennsylvania, November 28, 1841. Then the call "Move west young man, move west" again moved the family west. They settled in Salem Township of Steuben County. The farm where they lived is now within the city of Hudson, Indiana and some of the buildings are still standing and the two houses built by him are still occupied, one a wood frame, is still in the family. This house was being built for **Regina** at the time of her death in February 1875 and sets west of the barn. He later built a two story brick house just to the north of the barn. This area is still known today as the **Zongker** Farm and was featured in the late 1980"s or early 1990"s on a calender put out by the Bank of Ashley, Indiana.

Again the call to move struck. **John** went to Iowa. I have found some information that leads me to believe some of **John's** family may have gone on to South Dakota. **Henry** and family, along with **Joseph Martin's** daughter **Sarah** and her husband, **Levi Guthrie** and family, **Sarah's** brother, **Peter** moved southwest to Kansas, settling in western Reno and eastern Stafford counties. I was asked once what I knew about this family walking from Indiana to Kansas. All I can say is it is possible. I do know they had wagons as I was given a mule shoe as a teenager and was told by my father it was worn by Molly the mule that helped pull one of the wagons from Indiana.

Here is the picture of **Zonker** & Main, Hudson, Indiana, taken by Rob Bale in Oct 1994. You will see the house with the letters **JMZ** in the background. Built by **JMZ** for **Regina** she died before it was finished. She died Feb. 1875. He then built the brick house. The plaque in the cable end of it shows 1875. The barn in the picture shows the south side of it. As I understood this is what is left of the original barn. In the pencil picture, it shows a retaining wall at the West end of the barn. Look closely enough at this picture and you can see the difference in the ground elevation.

MRS. ELIZA ANN MCCLISH

Daughter of **Jacob** and **Magdalena (Walbourer) Meyers**
Wife of **George C McClish.**
Mother of
John Henry McClish(1858-1928)*
Samuel Anderson McClish (1859-1897)*
George Douglas McClish (1861-1945)*
Dora Elizabeth McClish Stienbarger(1865-1929)*
Emma Alice McClish Iobe(1867-1930)*
Eliza Ellen McClish (1869 -1913
Sarah Etta McClish Rice(1873-1940
William Edwin McClish (1875-1964
Myrtle Edith McClish Metty(1880-1947
Freddie Charles McClish (1884- 1885

......

OBIT:

Eliza Ann, daughter of **Jacob** and **Magdalena Myers** was born near Tiffin, Seneca Co., Ohio, March 12, 1839, and died at her home near Mendon, August 25, 1916; aged 77 years, 5 months, 13 days. She was married to **Geo. C. McClish** on June 23 1857. Ten children came to bless their union, the youngest, **Freddie**, dying in infancy; nine left the home roof to establish homes of their own; seven remain to mourn the mother's loss; two, **Samuel** and Mrs. **Ella Happle (Happel)** having passed to the great beyond.

On June 14, 1862, she, with her husband and little family came from Illinois and located on the farm where they since resided. She has seen the surrounding country change from a wilderness to fertile farms.

Hers was a beautiful life ever serving her family, giving advice and aid in her children's homes until the past few years it became necessary for the children to return some of the services owing to her age and poor health, and she was the recipient of the most devoted care from her children. She was confined to her bed the past few weeks and patiently awaited the end of a long life of loving service.

She is survived by a sorrowing husband, three sons--**John**, **George D.** and **William;** four daughters--Mrs. **Dora Stienbarger**, Mrs. **Alice Iobe**, Mrs. **Etta Rice**, Mrs. **Myrtle Metty.** All of whom live near the old home. She also leaves twenty-two grandchildren, ten great grand children, one great great grandchild, one brother, one sister, several half brothers and sisters. The funeral was conducted at the Wakeshma church on Sunday afternoon, August 27, by **Rev. G. E. Wright**, burial in the Beard cemetery.

Grand Rapids Press, February 28, 1935, (pg 23),
Thursday

Obituaries:
CASSELMAN – Bessie Casselman, aged 36, passed
away yesterday early Thursday morning at the
residence, 303 Straight Ave, S.W.; Surviving are the
husband, **Roy**, four sons – **Gene, Leroy, Walter** and
Howard. The body was removed to Greenhoe's
Home for funeral. Services will be held in the chapel,
Saturday afternoon at 2 o'clock. Interment in
Greenwood Cemetery.

Grand Rapids Press, August 16, 1957, (pg 32),
Thursday

Obituaries-

CASSELMAN- Leroy Casselman, aged 61, of 852
Watson, SW, passed away Wednesday afternoon at
 St. Mary's Hospital. His is survived by his widow,
Nellie, his mother, Mrs. **James Dinger**, of
Kalamazoo, Mich.; four sons: **Walter Casselman**, of
South Haven, Mich., **Leroy Casselman**, of Cleveland,
Ohio, and **Howard** and **Eugene Casselman**, both of
Grand Rapids; one grandchild; a stepson, Dr. **Robert
Ludwig**, of Grand Rapids; three sisters: Mrs. **Birgue
McClish**, of Brampton, Mich.; Mrs. **Clark
Steinbarger**, of Mendon, Mich.; Mrs. **John Scott**, of

Marshall, Mich. Funeral Services will be held Saturday afternoon at 1:30 o'clock at the Hollebeck Funeral Home, 100 West Leonard St. The **Rev, Milton Swanson** officiating. Interment at Rosedale Memorial Park. **Mr. Casselman** reposes at the funeral home, where friends may meet the family from 7 to 9 p.m., Friday.

Marshall Evening Chronicle, Jult 13, 1951, Tuesday

"Fredonia News"   Sunday guests of Mr. and Mrs. **Clarence Thorndyke** were Mr. and Mrs. **Virgil Thorndyke** and family of Olivet, Mr. and Mrs. **Marvin Benjamin** and daughter of Marshall, and Mr. and Mrs. **Clark Steinbarger** of Mendon.   Mr. and Mrs. **Roy Casselman** of Grand Rapids will spend Tuesday night and Wednesday with Mr. and Mrs. **Clarence Thorndyke**.

 There was no daughter named **Jean Casselman** of **Roy** & **Bessie**'s. It was a mistake in the census.

It should be a son **Eugene** (1928-2007) He is in the Social Security Index, died 12-9-2007, resident of Union City, Branch Co., MI, burial at Bethel Twp., Snow Prairie Cemetery, next to **Roland Duane "Bill" Waller** (1932-1998)

It also appears 3 other children died before **Bessie: Ruth, Edith, & John**, along with **Thelma May**.

Ottawa Co. Marriage License, posted in Holland
(Mich) Evening Sentinel, March 29, 1958 **Nellie
Casselman**, age 51y, of Grand Rapids, and **Richard
A. Burman**, age 60y, of Hudsonville

Letter from **Etta Dinger** to her children this is typed
exactly as I have it in my copy:

Oct. 19, 1927

Dear Children all;
It is pretty white here this morning with frost but
looks as if it is going to be a nice day as well as
yesterday2 It was Clydes birthday grandma thought of
it many times hope you had a pleasant day2 many,
many more. Well we sent that sewing machine
yesterday at last, Mina's grand children or Stanleys
wifes kids rather chopped the cover of her old up for
kindling in Detroit 2 Dolly had the cover of her old
machine yet I think I told you she had a new Singer,
so Dollys and another family came last Sun. When we
was at a neighbors eating chicken dinner 2 brought
the covers with . Now Eva after you try it out write
XXXX 2 tell us what success you are having with it 2
I hope XXXXX15XXXXXXXXX if it helps you out
an you will think of Aunt Mina every time you use it,
she said she would write 2 tell you all about it too.
Well you asked about XXXXX Roys wife I think I
know something of her, she only lived across the
driveway north of us for 3 years, she is built about
like lucy was when they lived at Jennings, has blue
eyes 2 black hair isn't rad looking 2 is the mother of 4

163

children, left her man Jones here for Roy 2 took the
youngest firl 2 nest the oldes 1, the oldest as a boy her
man is still here in Kazoo back tender in a paper mill
saw him xxxother day on street, her names was Bessie
Morrison before she married her father 2 sister lives
up at the Rapids her mother is dead, yes she came
down here with Roy last spring but we don't speak,
Roy is welcome to come 2 stay as long as he wants to
but not her, he was home not long ago 2 will be again
after his gun for hunting season many of his things
are here yet. Bessie 2 family was here 2 weeks ago 2
Hosea McClish 2 family visiting, wish you folks was
closer too. Well Iva I will have to close if I get this out
in mail with shipping bill so write 2 tell me all about
it. Blessing from Mother 2 all. Dad is sleeping 2 it is
almost 10 o'clock 2 we haven't had breakfast yet so
excuse writing please.

Envelope:
From Etta Dinger
Kalamazoo, Mich
R. R. #1, Box 327

The end of Volume 1 of this series... There are many
more stories to tell... and they will be told but this is
all for now. There is also no index... I know this will
drive our Family Historian crazy but that is the way I
am doing these books. I wanted to keep the cost of
the books down so I will be publishing the stories a
few at a time. I hope you have enjoyed this volume.

www.ingramcontent.com/pod-product-compliance
Lightning Source LLC
Chambersburg PA
CBHW061344250726
48657CB00004B/1325